ELIZABETH I

SEMPER·EADEM·

Bta

Com

dūo

Regni

Apud westm'

ELIZABETH I

The golden reign of Gloriana

DAVID LOADES

THE NATIONAL ARCHIVES

First published in 2003 by

The National Archives, Kew, Richmond, Surrey TW9 4DU, UK

www.nationalarchives.gov.uk

The National Archives was formed when the Public Record Office and Historical
Manuscripts Commission combined in April 2003

A catalogue record for this book is available from the British Library

ISBN 1 903365 43 0

Designed by Penny Jones and Michael Morris, Brentford, Middlesex

Printed in the UK by Butler and Tanner Ltd, Frome, Somerset

ILLUSTRATIONS

Cover: Coronation portrait of Elizabeth I (detail; see p. 34); *Coram Rege* Roll, 1584
(detail; see p. 2); (background) last known letter by Elizabeth I, to Henri IV, 1603.

Half-title page: Detail from the famous 'rainbow' portrait of Elizabeth I (see p. 80).

Frontispiece: Illuminated initial membrane, with portrait of Elizabeth I, Court of King's
Bench: *Coram Rege* Roll (Easter Term, 1572). The King's Bench was the senior
common law court until 1875, dealing with criminal offences. The decorative initial 'P'
was the 'Placita' (plea) put before the Queen, who was (in theory) present at the court.
The portraits were commissioned by court officials from artists, and are unique,
though stylized, likenesses.

Title page: The second Great Seal of Elizabeth I, used during the second half of
her reign. It is far more elaborate than the first Great Seal and was engraved by the
miniaturist Nicholas Hilliard. This is the reverse side, showing the Queen on horse-
back, flanked by the motifs of her three realms: the Tudor Rose of England, the Harp
of Ireland, and the Fleur-de-lys of France.

Contents page: Illuminated initial membrane, with portrait of Elizabeth I, Court
of King's Bench: *Coram Rege* Roll (Easter Term, 1589).

Page x (facing Preface): Illuminated frontispiece, with portrait initial of Elizabeth I,
and border with flowers, arms of St George and royal arms within cartouche, from
an indenture between the Queen and the dean and canons of St George's Windsor,
for performance of statutes concerning the thirteen poor knights, 1559. Produced
in the year of her coronation, this is one of the earliest portraits of the Queen.

Contents

Series Note

Most of the key historic documents selected for this series are from the collections at The National Archives; a few are reproduced courtesy of other important national or private repositories.

Each key document is reproduced on a numbered double-page spread with an explanatory introduction placing it in context. (Selected pages or details have been chosen for lengthy items.) Transcripts, with modernized spellings and explanations of archaic words, are provided where necessary. All the documents featured on these spreads are cross-referenced in the main text.

If you would like to see the original documents at The National Archives at Kew, please see www.nationalarchives.gov.uk or phone 020 8392 5200 for information about how to obtain a free Reader's Ticket.

For further information about titles in the ENGLISH MONARCHS series or other publications from The National Archives, please send your name and address to:

Publications Marketing, FREEPOST SEA 7565, Richmond, Surrey, UK TW9 4DU
(stamp required from overseas)

To order any publication from The National Archives, visit www.pro.gov.uk/bookshop/

The Documents

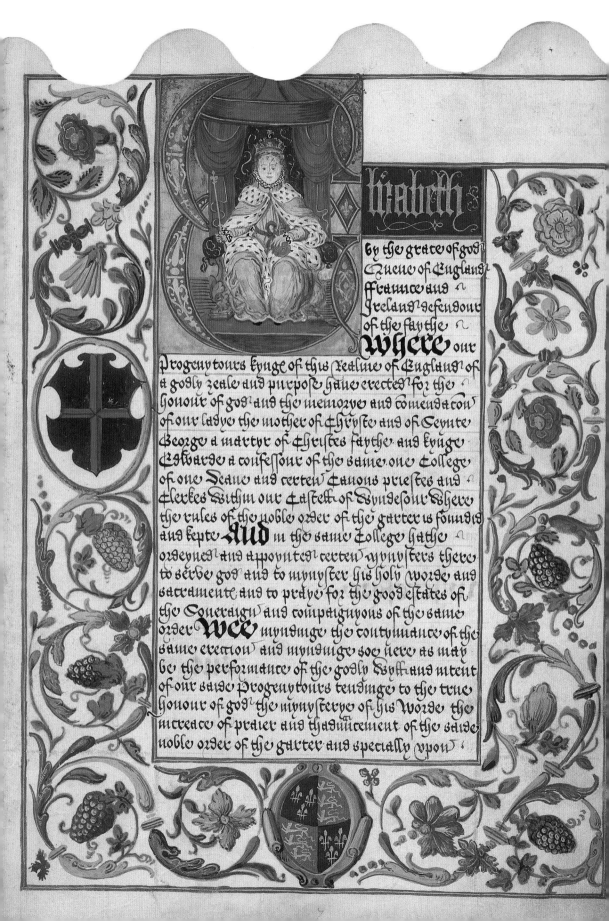

Elizabeth

by the grace of god
Quene of England
France and
Ireland defendour
of the faythe **Where** our
Progenytours kynge of this realme of England of
a godly zeale and purpose have erected for the
honour of god and the memorye and comendacow
of our ladye the mother of Chryste and of Seynte
George a martyr of Christes faythe and kynge
Edwarde a confessour of the same one College
of one Deane and certen Canons priestes and
Clerkes within our Castell of Wyndesour where
the rules of the noble order of the garter is founded
and kepte **And** in the same College hathe
ordeyned and appoynted certen mynysters there
to serve god and to mynyster his holy worde and
sacramente and to praye for the good estates of
the Soveraign and companyons of the same
order **Wee** myndinge the contynuance of the
same erection and myndinge soo here as may
be the performance of the godly wyll and intent
of our saide Progenytours tendinge to the true
honour of god the mynysterye of his worde the
increace of praier and thadvancement of the saide
noble order of the garter and specially upon

Preface

Elizabeth I died four hundred years ago, and this book marks that occasion. It does not pretend to be a biography, much less a study of the reign. It is a commemoration, partly in her own words, partly in the words of her servants and contemporaries, and partly in the words of one modern historian. The summary of her life and career is necessarily brief, the intention being to emphasize those aspects which now appear to have been particularly significant, either for herself or for the country over which she ruled.

England has had six female monarchs, and Great Britain four, including the joint rule of Mary II. It was determined by statute in the first year of Mary I (1554) that there was no distinction between male and female in respect of the powers of the Crown, and all ruling queens subsequently have enjoyed the benefit of that decision. Three of these ruling queens have enjoyed exceptionally long reigns, and two of them, Elizabeth I and Victoria, have given their names to the periods in which they ruled. The one who enjoyed the most power, as distinct from influence, was the one who did not marry, Elizabeth I. It is she more than any other who has attracted the attention of historians.

Elizabeth was not the greatest English monarch. In terms of achievement she was probably inferior to Henry II, Edward III, Henry VII, or even Charles II. But she was one of the greatest. Some problems she solved, and some were solved for her; she gave an identity and pride to her people; she gave a new direction to English enterprise, and her virginity became the symbol of her realm's integrity. Some problems she failed to solve, and they were to afflict her successors with disastrous consequences. She was the only *femme seule* ever to have reigned in England or Great Britain, and that has been part of her legend. Nevertheless, Elizabeth the Legend and Elizabeth the Queen are not quite the same thing, and it is part of the purpose of this book to disentangle the two. Elizabeth's motto was 'Always the Same', but historical perceptions change, and this is a view from the beginning of the twenty-first century.

The Young Elizabeth

THE KING'S 'GREAT MATTER'

Elizabeth was born in September 1533, probably the most eagerly anticipated royal child of the century. To conceive her in wedlock, her father Henry VIII had been forced to annul his first marriage, a process which had drawn him and his kingdom into an elaborate and dangerous political maze.

Henry's first Queen, Catherine of Aragon, had borne only one child who had survived infancy, their daughter Mary. By 1527 Catherine was past her childbearing years, and Henry desperately wanted a son. For about five years he tried every kind of pleading and political manoeuvering to persuade Pope Clement VII to grant his wish to be free from Catherine. But Clement was dominated by the Emperor Charles V, who was Catherine's nephew, and Henry found his every move frustrated. Catherine might have retired

Illuminated initial membrane, with portrait of Elizabeth I, Court of King's Bench: *Coram Rege* Roll (Easter Term, 1584).

Greenwich Palace, Elizabeth's birthplace, from the north bank of the Thames. From 'The Panorama of London' c. 1544, by Anthonis van den Wyngaerde.

gracefully into a nunnery if Henry had not conducted himself so clumsily, and if he had not made it clear that he had already identified Catherine's successor in the person of Anne Boleyn. The Queen refused to give way to another woman, and contested the King at every turn. By the end of 1532 Henry had decided that he would have to seek a solution without reference to the Pope. Anne Boleyn became pregnant, and the King secretly married her. In the

Elizabeth's mother, Anne Boleyn. Artist unknown.

Title page of the *Valor Ecclesiasticus*, 1535, a survey and valuation of Church wealth in England and Wales. It showed Henry what he would inherit as Head of the English Church, and the Dissolution of the Monasteries began the following year.

spring of 1533 a judgement by the new Archbishop of Canterbury, Thomas Cranmer, declared that Henry was not, and never had been, married to Catherine; his second marriage was therefore lawful, and the child Anne was carrying would be legitimate. This judgement in defiance of the papal curia forced Henry to repudiate papal jurisdiction altogether in the following year, and he called upon Parliament to give his action the full force of English law.

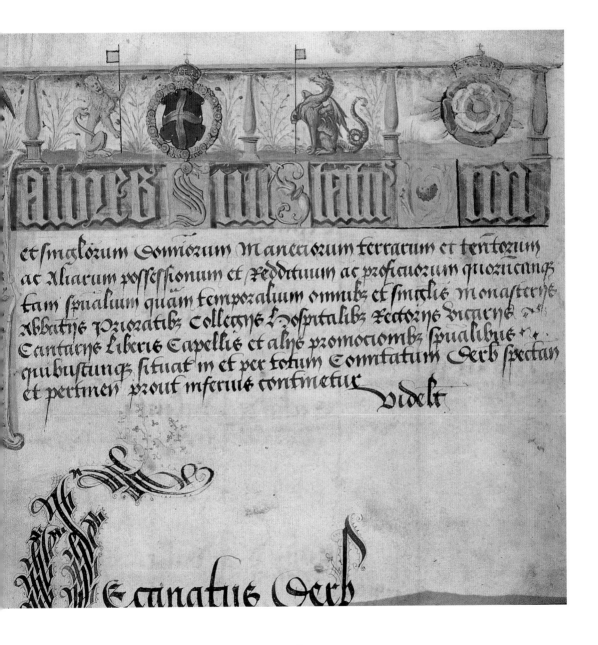

The schism which had thus arisen for purely political reasons swiftly became entangled with demands for ecclesiastical reform, which were much easier to realize in a Church which no longer owed allegiance to a theologically conservative papacy. When Elizabeth was born, therefore, she was at the same time both a bitter disappointment and a symbol of a new era. She was a disappointment because of her sex: having moved heaven and earth to get a legitimate son, Henry was left with another daughter. His enemies could scarcely conceal their glee, and the King was forced to put his 'divine approval' propaganda on hold. On the other hand he had no intention of giving up, either on procreation or on his ecclesiastical programme. Elizabeth was recognized as his heir, and the Church became dominated by the evangelical programme of the New Learning. This was not doctrinally Protestant, but shared many of the reformers' priorities, particularly those for education and the translation of the scriptures into English. Anne Boleyn was a leader and patron of this evangelical movement, and her daughter thus became a symbol of its success, as well as of the repudiation of the Pope.

The indictment against Anne Boleyn and her brother George, Lord Rochford, for high treason, adultery and incest. This is a record from the court of the Lord High Steward and Peers: a specially commissioned court which had the particular function of trying peers accused of treason. The other defendants charged with high treason and adultery with Anne – courtiers Mark Smeaton, Henry Norris, William Brereton and Sir Francis Weston – were tried separately.

In 1536, however, this situation was ruined by Henry's egotism and credulity. Anne's spirited independence, which had fascinated him in a mistress, irritated him profoundly in a wife. He became suspicious of her lively sexuality, and began to listen to those who were warning him that her failure to bear a son was another divine judgement. In February 1536 she miscarried of a male child, and the King's suspicions grew darker. Catherine had died in January, and he was therefore no longer under any pressure to return to her. He began to contemplate the possibility of removing Anne, and starting again. He had his eye on another young lady, Jane Seymour, but would probably not have acted in the way he did if Anne's numerous political enemies had not succeeded in poisoning

his mind. He became convinced, on the most circumstantial evidence, that she was guilty of adultery, incest and witchcraft; the latter, of course being an exculpation for the influence which she had exercised over him for nearly a decade. When the King had made up his mind in this fashion, the judicial process was a mere formality, and Anne was executed in May, her marriage to the King having been formally judged null and void. Before her third birthday Elizabeth had, therefore, joined her half sister Mary in the limbo status of 'the King's natural daughter'. Her education had not yet begun, and she would barely have remembered her mother; yet she carried in her genes that wit, independent spirit, and propensity for sexual display which had brought Anne to both triumph and disaster.

SCHOLARLY PROMISE

As a small child, Elizabeth would not have noticed her change of status. She suffered no deprivation, and if she was surrounded with less ceremony and a smaller entourage than she would have enjoyed as a princess, that can hardly have mattered to her. Her material needs were well cared for, and when her brother Edward was born in 1537 she was placed with her personal servants in the context of the grand household which was created for him. She performed her first public duty at his christening, bearing the Chrisom cloth, which was wrapped around the child's head to absorb the anointing oil. She was herself carried in the arms of her step-uncle, the Earl of Hertford. By that time she was learning her first letters under the guidance of a young woman who was to become her lifelong friend and mentor, Catherine Champernowne, better known by her later married name of Catherine ('Kat') Ashley. Catherine was the daughter of Sir Philip Champernowne, a Devon gentleman of some culture and learning, and belonged herself to that educated humanist circle with which the King was surrounded during the ascendancy of Thomas Cromwell. That circle proved more durable than the minister himself. Although he fell from power in the summer of 1540, by the time Edward's education was seriously taken in hand in 1543, it had regrouped around the person of Henry's last Queen, Catherine Parr.

By then there is plentiful testimony to the fact that Catherine Champernowne had made a good job of Elizabeth's primary education. She could read and write fluently in English, and had a sound grounding in the universal language of learning, Latin. She was also alert, inquisitive, and well mannered. In 1544, as a result of Catherine's contacts (through her brother-in-law Anthony Denny, a Gentleman of the King's Privy Chamber) with St John's College, Cambridge, William Grindal took over her responsibilities as tutor. This was no reflection on Catherine, but she was aware of her own limitations, and of the exceptional talents which her pupil was displaying. Grindal was an excellent scholar in both Latin and Greek, and a skilful and sympathetic teacher. He also remained closely in touch with his own tutor,

Princess Elizabeth, aged about fifteen. Artist unknown.

An orpharian reputedly made for Elizabeth by John Rose, in 1580. Like her father, Elizabeth was very musical, and was accomplished on the virginals and lute.

Catherine Parr, Henry VIII's sixth (and last) wife. Artist unknown.

Roger Ascham, who was appointed to teach the young Prince Edward at the same time. It is from Ascham's memoirs that we learn most of the eleven-year-old Elizabeth's remarkable precocity. A little also survives of her own work. In July 1544 she wrote a letter to her stepmother in careful and elegant Italian. It was a school exercise, and there is no evidence that Catherine Parr could read Italian, but it demonstrated Elizabeth's skill. Grindal was not teaching her Italian, and her tutor for this purpose was probably Jean Baptiste Castiglione, who was to remain in her service for many years. At the end of December 1545, when she was twelve, she sent Catherine a translation of Calvin's *Institutes* from French into English, accompanied by a letter in French; and to her father a Latin version of the Queen's 'Prayers and meditations', accompanied by an elegant letter in the same language. By this time she was fluent in Latin, French and Italian, and had made good progress with Greek. Document 1, *Elizabeth the scholar* demonstrates the Princess's early academic achievements.

THE SEYMOUR AFFAIR

Elizabeth underwent three major emotional crises in her life, each of which affected her subsequent behaviour. The first was her encounter with Thomas Seymour, which lasted for about eighteen months in 1547–8, either side of her fifteenth birthday. The second was her imprisonment after Sir Thomas Wyatt's rebellion in 1554, when she spent several months in the Tower, in daily fear of trial and execution for high treason. The third was her love affair with Robert Dudley; as a crisis that lasted for about two years from 1559 to 1561, but its after-effects went on for as long as Lord Robert was alive, and perhaps longer.

Thomas Seymour was the younger brother of Edward, Earl of Hertford, who became Duke of Somerset and Lord Protector after the death of Henry VIII in 1547. In 1547 he was a man approaching forty, with a moderately successful political and military career already behind him. He was also a personable man, of great charm, and with a streak of recklessness in him which gave him powerful sex appeal. It was believed that he had been about to marry Catherine Parr when her second husband, Lord Latimer, died, but the King had beaten him to it. When Catherine became available again in January 1547, Seymour wasted no time in laying siege to her. She was still only in her mid-thirties, and had suffered three impotent or elderly husbands. It is not surprising, therefore, that she responded swiftly and eagerly to these welcome advances, and the couple were secretly married in April. The Protector reacted angrily, both because he felt that Catherine had moved with indecent haste, and also because the Council's permission for the union should have been sought. Seymour was unabashed, but his relations with his brother began to deteriorate.

At the time when this was happening, both Mary and Elizabeth were living in Catherine's household, and such was Seymour's reputation that he was rumoured to have made a pass at each of the Princesses before settling on their stepmother. Mary, who at this point was thirty-one, immediately removed herself and set up her own establishment, but Elizabeth remained with

1 *Elizabeth the scholar*

One of Elizabeth's earliest surviving letters, written when she was eleven, to her stepmother, Queen Catherine (Parr). The six-page letter is in her own hand and displays the kind of modesty that was regarded at the time as simply good manners.

The letter, dated 31 December 1544, accompanied a New Year's gift: Elizabeth's own English translation of Marguerite of Angoulême's *Miroir de l'ame Pecheresse*. This translation was a school exercise, designed to demonstrate Elizabeth's skill in French. Marguerite was the humanist sister of François I of France, and the choice of this work reflects not only the tastes of Elizabeth's tutors, but also those of Catherine herself, who was later to emerge as a strong Protestant. The translation may have been made from the 1533 edition of the *Miroir*, which had been in Anne Boleyn's library. Elizabeth's work was later amended by John Bale and published at Marburg in 1548.

The exchange of New Year's gifts was a major court ritual. Whereas the monarch received a wide variety of objects, including cash, the presents given in return invariably consisted of pieces of silver gilt plate. What Elizabeth received on this occasion is not recorded. Earlier recorded gifts by Elizabeth had been pieces of needle-work presented to her brother Edward.

The fact that this letter was written at all suggests that Elizabeth was not at court at the end of 1544.

ELIZABETH WROTE:

To our most noble and virtuous Queen Catherine, Elizabeth, her humble daughter, wishes perpetual felicity and everlasting joy.

Not only knowing the affectuous [earnest] will and fervent zeal which your highness has towards all godly learning, as also my duty towards you (most gracious and sovereign princess); but knowing also that pusillanimity and idleness are most repugnant unto a reasonable creature, and that (as the philosopher [Aristotle] says) even as an instrument of iron

The letter continues:

or other metal waxes soon rusty unless it be continually occupied, even so shall the wit of a man or woman wax dull and unapt [unfit] to do or understand anything perfectly unless it be always occupied upon some manner of study. Which things considered has moved so small a portion as God has lent me to prove what I could do. And therefore have I (as for assay or beginning, following the right notable saying of the proverb aforesaid) translated this little book out of French rhyme into English prose, joining the sentences together as well as the capacity of my simple wit and small learning could extend themselves. The which book is entitled or named *The Mirror* or *Glass of the Sinful Soul*, wherein is contained how she (beholding and contemplating what she is) does perceive how of herself and of her own strength she can do nothing that is good or prevails for her salvation, unless it be through the grace of God, whose mother, daughter, sister and wife by the Scriptures she proves herself to be. Trusting also that through His incomprehensible love, grace and mercy, she (being called from sin to repentance) does faithfully hope to be saved.

And although I know that, as for my part which I have wrought in it (as well spiritual as manual), there is nothing done as it should be, nor else worthy to come in your grace's hands, but rather all unperfect and uncorrect; yet do I trust also that, howbeit [though] it is like a work which is but new begun and shapen, that the file of your excellent wit and Godly learning in the reading of it, if so it vouchsafe your highness to do, shall rub out, polish, and mend (or else cause to mend) the words (or rather the order of my writing), the which I know in many places to be rude and nothing done as it should be. But I hope that after to have been in your grace's hands, there shall be nothing in it worthy of reprehension, and that in the mean-while no other but your highness only shall read it or see it, lest my faults be known of many. Then shall they be better excused (as my confidence is in your grace's accustomed benevolence) than if I should bestow a whole year in writing or inventing ways for to excuse them. Praying God Almighty, the maker and creator of all things, to grant unto your highness the same New Year's Day a lucky and a prosperous year, with prosperous issue and continuance of many years in good health and continual joy and all to His honour, praise and glory.

From Ashridge [her house in Hertfordshire] the last day of the year of our Lord God 1544.

TO OVR MOST NOBLE AND
vertuous quene KATHERIN, Eliza
beth, her humble daughter, wisheth
perpetuall felicitie, and euerlasting ioye

NOT ONELY knowing the affe
ctuous wille, and feruent zeale, the
wich your highnes hath towardes
all godly lerning, as also my dueti
towardes you (most gracious and
souueraine princes) but knowing also that
pusilanimite and idlenes are most
repugnant vnto a reasonable crea
ture, and that (as the philosopher
sayeth) euen as an instrument of yron

Catherine and her new husband. Thomas proceeded to give his young charge what can only be described as a sexual education, and in that he was abetted, somewhat improbably, by Catherine Ashley. There were romps and horseplay, in which Ashley seemed to see no harm, perhaps because Catherine Parr herself was often involved. She may even have felt that it was a golden opportunity to teach this sheltered and bookish child some of the facts of life. Royal princesses were normally so protected from undesireable males that they ended up being thrown into the marriage bed without the slightest idea of what was about to happen. Not so Elizabeth. These jolly games, however, came to an abrupt end when the Queen Dowager found her husband embracing his charge in compromising circumstances. The couple had a furious row and Elizabeth was sent away in disgrace. Read a letter written by Elizabeth around this time: document 2, *Formal courtesies*.

There the matter might have ended, had it not been for the fact that Catherine died in childbirth in 1548. No sooner was she safely buried than Seymour began to renew his attentions to Elizabeth, and this time the magic word 'marriage' was mentioned. There are numerous signs that the young Princess had found her awakening as exhilarating as it had been perilous. Seymour was just the man to turn a young girl's head; however, talk of marriage was dangerous. She was the King's sister, and her disposal in that mode was an affair of State, not of whim, or even of lust. Catherine Ashley, although she still favoured Seymour, became cautious. According to the testimony which she later gave, and which Elizabeth corroborated, they spoke frequently of the possibility of marriage with Seymour, and even joked and teased each other about it, but always with the proviso 'if the Council permits'.

There was not the slightest chance that the Council would permit. Seymour's hubris, and his jealousy of his brother were making him a dangerous man. He was building up support in the House of Lords, apparently for a political attack upon the Protector, and was rumoured to be arming his servants and retainers. In January 1549 he was arrested, and one of the charges against him was plotting to marry the King's sister. The rumours began to fly: he had seduced Elizabeth; she was with child by him; she was herself under arrest. Both the Princess and Catherine Ashley were rigorously interrogated (see Catherine's statement, document 3, *Trouble with Thomas Seymour*). Elizabeth wrote a remarkably mature and composed letter to the Lord Protector, protesting against the 'shameful slanders' which were reflecting upon her honour. She was fifteen, and had learned painfully about the impact of her personal behaviour upon her social and political circumstances. She had also learned that she was an attractive young woman, who had almost as interesting an effect upon men as they had upon her. Seymour paid for his indiscretions (of which this was only one) with his life; Elizabeth suffered no worse consequences than the loss for a few months of her friend and mentor. Catherine Ashley was held to have acted with negligence and indiscretion, and was dismissed; it was the autumn of 1549 before she was allowed to return. It appears that Elizabeth's infatuation with Thomas Seymour was just that, an adolescent crush. She was appropriately saddened by his death, but it seems to have made no significant impact upon her.

Thomas Seymour, Lord Seymour of Sudeley; Lord Admiral. Artist unknown.

2 *Formal courtesies*

A letter of thanks from Elizabeth to Edward Seymour, Duke of Somerset and Lord Protector. It was clearly written after Elizabeth withdrew from the household of the Protector's brother, Thomas Seymour, following the scandal in their relationship, and may date from around September 1548. Although it is signed by Elizabeth, who was then about fifteen, the body of the letter is in a clerk's hand.

Edward Seymour, as Earl of Hertford, had been a leading member of Henry VIII's Council in the last years of the reign. The dispositions made in the King's will gave him the opportunity, early in February 1547, to stage what was effectively a coup d'état, whereby he was constituted Duke and Protector. He was also made Governor of the King's Person for the young Edward VI, who was nine at the time of his father's death. Somerset's relations with Elizabeth were amicable, partly because of their shared Protestant convictions.

The nature of Elizabeth's 'sickness' referred to in this letter is unknown, but it does not seem to have been serious; the 'Doctor Bill' who treated her was one of a number of Royal Physicians on the regular payroll of the Chamber. The 'patent' mentioned was the grant of the estate ordered for Elizabeth under the terms of her father's will, which did not finally take effect until 1551. Cheshunt, where Elizabeth wrote the letter, was the home of Sir Anthony Denny (former Chief Gentleman of Henry VIII's Privy Chamber) and his wife Joan (née Champernowne, the sister of Elizabeth's friend and mentor Catherine Ashley).

ELIZABETH WROTE:

My very good lord

Many lines will not serve to render the least part of the thanks that your grace has deserved of me, most especially for that you have been careful for my health, sending unto me not only your comfortable [comforting] letters, but also physicians as Doctor Bill, whose diligence and pain has been a great part of my recovery. For whom I do most heartily thank your grace, desiring you to give him thanks for me, who can ascertain you of my state of health, wherefore I will not write it. And although I be most bound to you in this time of my sickness, yet I may not be unthankful for that your grace has made such expedition for my patent. With most hearty thanks and commendations to you and to my good lady your wife, most heartily fare you well. From Cheshunt this present Friday.

Your assured friend to my power, Elizabeth.

④

76
148

My deare good Lord many lynes will not serve to
render the least part of the thanks that yowr grace hath
deserved off me most especially for that you have byn
carefull for my health and sending vnto me not only
yowr comfortable letters but also physicyans as Doctor
Byll whose diligens and paine hath ben a great pte
off my recovery for whom I do most hartly thank yowr
grace desyryng you to gyve him thankes for me who
can vnfeyning you off myne estate off health wherfor
I will not write it And allthough I be most bound
to you in this tyme off my sicknes yet I may not
be vnthankfull for that yowr grace hath made
expedycyon for my patent is my most harty thankes
and comendacyons to you and to my good lady yowr
wife most hartly fare you well from Cortham
this present fryday

Fryday 8
15
22

yowr assuryd frende to
my power

Elizabeth

24

9

3 Trouble with Thomas Seymour

The first of three examinations of Catherine Ashley following the arrest of Thomas Seymour, the Lord Admiral, in January 1549. Each is written in the hand of Sir Thomas Smith, the Principal Secretary, but it is not known which other members of the Council were involved in her questioning. This particular document extends to two pages.

In all three interrogations, Catherine gives the impression that she favoured Seymour and encouraged his advances, but she may have been protecting her charge. She refers to Seymour in the second paragraph as 'your old husband, that was appointed to you' which is an allusion to the rumour that Henry had 'appointed' (or arranged) for Elizabeth to marry Seymour. There is no evidence for this, and the remark was probably a jocular reference to Elizabeth's 'fancy'. Catherine certainly had a guilty conscience about her role, although she insisted that she and Elizabeth both agreed that marriage, which was a matter of State, could only have taken place with the consent of the Protector.

Catherine Willoughby was the second wife of Charles Brandon, Duke of Suffolk, who had died in 1545. She was a staunch Protestant and a friend of Elizabeth's.

Thomas Parry was Elizabeth's cofferer, and it was through him that Seymour had offered Elizabeth the use of his London house and its contents until she had secured a residence of her own. Seymour may have had an ulterior motive in doing this, or it may have been simple courtesy.

Ultimately, Seymour was executed by his brother for treason but Catherine's examinations were not specifically used against him. Elizabeth herself was both angry and distressed about what had happened, but she never admitted to any wrong doing and was not in any personal danger.

SIR THOMAS SMITH WROTE:

February 2, 1548[9]. The answers of Mistress Ashley. What communication she has had with my Lady Elizabeth's grace as touching the marriage with the Lord Admiral.

She said that incontinent [immediately] after the death of the queen, at Cheshunt the lady Elizabeth was sick. She [Ashley] said unto her 'Your old husband, that was appointed to you at the death of the king [Henry VIII] now is free again. You may have him if you will.'

And she answered 'no'.

Then said Mistress Ashley 'I wis [know well] you will not deny it if my Lord Protector and the Council were pleased thereunto'.

And one there answered, 'She cannot see who'. (Addressing Elizabeth) 'And why not him that was worthy to match a queen should not marry with you?'

And at divers other times when she [Elizabeth] had been at play in drawing hands, she had seen my Lord Admiral and my lady of Suffolk [Catherine Willoughby, the dowager duchess] together. And when she had chosen my Lord Admiral, she would laugh and pale at it. And then this examinate [Ashley] would say, 'I wis you would not refuse him if the Council would be content thereunto'. And then at the death of the Queen, it was reported that my Lord Admiral was the heaviest [saddest] man in the world, and this examinate would her [Elizabeth] to write or cause her secretary to write to comfort him, and she to subscribe.

The document continues:

Her grace answered she would not, for then she should be thought to woo him.

Item. Upon [Thomas] Parry's letter, wherein he [Thomas Seymour] offered his house and household stuff and this examinate gave her counsel to refuse both except Mr. [Anthony] Denny would give advice unto it; whereupon she [Elizabeth] bade this examinate so to answer, and so she [Ashley] did (send) Thomas Parry some word that the Lord Admiral would see her grace as he rode; whereupon this examinate wrote again that in no wise [event] he should come there until the said Lord Admiral should come to that parliament again, and then this examinate would come to London and tell him her mind.

Another time, about Allhallowtide [1 November], she [Ashley] asked leave to go to London, and being demanded of her grace what she would do there, she answered that she would speak with my Lord Admiral. Her grace that she should not, for it would be said that she [Elizabeth] did send her. This errand was to have begged the gatekeeper at Durham Place [Seymour's London house] for herself [Ashley], for she had no good lodging nor house in London.

2° feb. 1548

The examynacõn of Mr. asshley

What Comm̃nes she hath had w[i]t[h] my
Lad[ie] Elizabeth yeam ab[out] tow[chyn]g the
Marr[iag]e w[i]t[h] the L. Admyrall

She sayth that furthwith after the death of the
quen at Chelsey / weys the sayd lady Eliz.
was att / She said but her if the Comm̃sta
[...] to shew ... ould husband that was
apoynted but ye at the death of the kyng nom
is her agayn / you may haue hym if you wold
And she dysdainid nay / She sayd
what she: that you will not knowe it
if my L. p[ro]tect[o]r [...] Comm̃sta how
pleast though / And ... this awswerd
she say wel ... And what her yf noob works
to marryge a q[uen] shall not marrie w[i]t[h]
yow / And at diu[er]s other tymes
weys she hath byn at glace she deuysyng
haue she hath for my L. Ad ... my L. of
p[er]fect togeer whyes she hath oft[en] my
L. Ad she wold laughe & pass at it / And
sayd that ye wold say Trust you wold ne
... her yf she wayted wold be shew
theras /
And ther on the day of the Comm̃ she was
Reportyng that my L. d[itto] was the ... was in
the worlde / & that ye ... wold hie to writ or
cause his secretary to writt, & she & she sabsche

51

Ratclyffe
[signature]

O mercyfull god
do vs not forsake.

& make ó hart brnk
to leeve in thy ffth.

Though of thmgs for god
Oft tymes ye be sake.

But alwaye kenke
ó king realme a save.

Apud westm̃ Tanm̃

A Queen in the Making

SISTER TO THE KING

William Grindal had died young in 1548 and for the next few years Roger Ascham, one of the best-known teachers of his generation, directed Elizabeth's studies. Under his guidance she studied the New Testament in Greek, and by the time he returned to Cambridge in 1550 she was a thoroughly accomplished scholar, fluent in five languages, and well seen in theology, philosophy and history. By this time she was seventeen, and her formal schooling seems to have come to an end, leaving her not only the best educated woman of her generation, but also one of the few members of the royal family ever to develop genuine intellectual tastes and abilities.

Elizabeth was also a Protestant. Under the guidance of such mentors as Grindal, Ascham and John Cheke, like many others brought up in the New Learning, she moved swiftly to embrace reformed doctrines once her formidable father was no more. Her brother Edward famously did the same, and his convictions set the tone for his reign. We cannot set a date for the conversion of either of them, and it is probable that Edward, who was only nine when his father died, was never taught orthodox Catholic doctrine at all. Whether Elizabeth ever held traditional views on justification or the sacraments we do not know, but if she did, she had abandoned them by 1549. She was also at this time noted for a puritanical simplicity of dress, and the absence of personal adornment, although whether this was from her own choice, or out of a desire to please her increasingly puritanical brother, is not known.

Illuminated initial membrane, with portrait of Edward VI,
Court of King's Bench: *Coram Rege* Roll (Easter Term, 1546).

In 1551, at the age of eighteen, she took seisin – that is legal possession – of her own estates. Like Mary, she then became a magnate in her own right. Her Chamber was now managed by the faithful Catherine Ashley; William Cecil became her surveyor, and she saw quite a lot of her childhood friend Robert Dudley, the son of John Dudley, Earl of Warwick, who by that time was chief minister as

Henry VIII and his family (detail). Henry is flanked by his son Edward and Edward's mother, Jane Seymour – even though Jane died shortly after Edward's birth.

President of the Council. Robert was newly married to Amy Robsart, the daughter of a Norfolk knight, and there was no hint of any close relationship with the Princess, but both were regularly at court. The young King seems to have been genuinely fond of both his sisters, but with Mary (who was old enough to be his mother) he fell out seriously over the question of the Mass. By 1549 Mary

Princess Mary is on the left of the portrait, and Princess Elizabeth is on the right. Artist unknown.

was *persona non grata* and constantly at loggerheads with the minority Council, but Elizabeth was welcome, and spent quite a lot of time in Edward's company. They had much in common, and not just in their religious convictions.

So good was their relationship that it must have come as a severe shock to her to discover in June 1553 that she had been excluded from the order of succession to the throne. Ten years earlier Henry's last Succession Act had, in addition to confirming Edward's status as his heir, decreed that if Edward should die without children of his own, the Crown was to descend first to Mary and then to Elizabeth. The illegitimacy of both was simply ignored, and no one disputed that Parliament had the right to determine the succession in this manner. The Act also authorized Henry to confirm or amend its terms by his own last will and testament. At the beginning of January 1547 he had confirmed them. In view of Mary's defiant religious stand, and the seriousness with which Edward took his 'Godly Reformation', it was not surprising that, when his health suddenly collapsed in June 1553, he should have made an attempt to exclude Mary. But why his Godly sister Elizabeth as well?

The reason seems to have been that Edward, perhaps prompted by his mentor, John Dudley, did not want to make an issue of religion, perhaps for fear of creating a precedent. The issue was legitimacy. It was implied, but not clearly stated, that statute did not have the power to ignore legitimacy in determining the succession, because that form of inheritance was a part of Divine Law. Fond as he was of Elizabeth, Edward believed that her mother had been guilty as charged, and that she was consequently the child of a non-marriage. This consistency was not, however, extended to the other clauses of the Act, which was followed in the exclusion of the legitimate Stuart line, which should have come next if strict primogeniture had been applied. In the event, the young King tried to settle his Crown by Letters Patent upon his particular friend Jane Grey. Jane was the eldest daughter of Frances Grey, Duchess of Suffolk

Roll from the special commission of *oyer et terminer* (to hear and determine). This sets out the charges against Lady Jane Grey, Archbishop Cranmer, Guildford Dudley, Sir Ambrose Dudley, and Henry Dudley, of high treason and the assumption of royal authority by Lady Jane Grey. Mary pardoned many of Jane's followers, and was reluctant to have Jane and her husband, Guildford Dudley, executed. Nevertheless, they were beheaded in February 1554, in the aftermath of the Wyatt rebellion.

and granddaughter of Henry's younger sister Mary by her second marriage to Charles Brandon. She was a staunch Protestant, and recently married (much against her will) to Guildford Dudley, John's youngest son. She was about two years younger than Elizabeth and, like her, was highly educated.

SISTER TO THE QUEEN

There was little law or logic to justify this action, and when Edward died on 6 July 1553, Jane's position quickly crumbled away. Within a fortnight she and her main supporters were in the Tower, and Mary was on the throne. Elizabeth reacted to the news of her brother's death by assembling a substantial force of 2,000 horsemen, which was a remarkable tribute to the size of her affinity. In the event all this cavalry did was escort her to London to share in her sister's triumph; so which side it would have been engaged upon in the event of serious fighting, we do not know. Probably she would have supported Mary to the best of her ability, however suspicious she may have been of her religion, because it was in her interest to uphold her father's Succession Act. She might have been comfortable in a country ruled by Queen Jane, but there would have been little future for her.

Queen Mary I of England, 1554, by Anthonis Mor.

Illuminated initial membrane, with portrait of Mary I, Court of King's Bench: *Coram Rege* Roll (Michaelmas Term, 1553).

The 'sisters together' act did not last very long. Despite her tolerant public statements, Mary soon made it clear that Protestantism was poison in her sight, and that everyone at court would have to go to Mass, whether they liked it or not. Elizabeth did not like it. She was evasive and genuinely distressed, but she could not afford to be defiant if she wished to survive. Unlike Mary in similar circumstances, she was not backed by a formidable foreign power, and after several weeks of diplomatic illness, she conformed. Neither the Queen nor anyone else believed that she was really converted, but in the face of such compliance there was little more to be done. Elizabeth attended the coronation, and then withdrew to her estates.

If there had ever been any cordiality in the relationship between the two women, it had completely disappeared by October 1553. Charles V's ambassador, Simon Renard, who was Mary's closest confidant in the first year of her reign, believed that Elizabeth was heading a secret Protestant resistance movement, and that she was in the pocket of the King of France. The Queen in turn made it clear that she had every intention of excluding her sister from the succession, partly because she did not trust her religion, and partly because she was too much like her mother! These were perceptive observations, but the threatened exclusion never happened; unless or until Mary produced an alternative, Elizabeth was the last hope of the Tudor dynasty. The Queen took the obvious step of planning to marry, although her initial popularity declined steeply when it became known that her intended was Philip, Prince of Spain, the only legitimate son of the Emperor Charles V. Elizabeth's name was soon on the lips of every malcontent. To what extent she was really involved in the conspiracy and rebellion which then followed is still uncertain. The conspirators almost certainly approached her, and some fringe members of her affinity took part; consequently she could legitimately have been charged with misprision of treason for concealing her knowledge, but it is highly unlikely that she made any move herself, or had any direct contact with the rebels. Nevertheless Renard was convinced of her guilt, and persuaded Mary, at least to the extent of ordering her arrest, which took place in February 1554, a few days after the rising had collapsed.

Illuminated initial membrane, with portrait of Queen Mary and Philip II, Court of King's Bench: *Coram Rege* Roll (Hilary Term, 1558).

Our knowledge of what followed is heavily dependent upon the partisan account of John Foxe, written after Elizabeth's accession, but the basic facts are not in dispute. When the Councillors arrived to escort her to court, she professed sickness. They had clearly anticipated this move, since they had brought two of the royal physicians with them, who pronounced her fit to travel; she was moved, gently but firmly, from Ashridge to London, accompanied by much theatrical lamentation. At court, she was left to cool her heels, and build up her anxiety, for several days before her interrogation began. She wept, denied all guilt, and professed undying loyalty to her sister. Neither Mary nor her servants were impressed, and on 18 March the Princess was carried as a prisoner to the Tower. She pleaded hard against this open shame, but succeeded only in delaying her incarceration for one day (read Elizabeth's plea to Mary, document 4, *Elizabeth in danger*). Although she put on a good act of injured innocence, it is clear that she was terrified by these threatening moves, as well she might be. Renard was doing his best to persuade Mary that Philip could never be safe in England if Elizabeth remained alive; the Lord Chancellor, Stephen Gardiner, was also working for her trial and conviction. Fortunately for her, she also had friends, even within the Privy Council, the chief of whom at this stage was Lord Paget. They succeeded in blocking each

The L. Elizabeth Prisoner in the Tower

The L. Elizabeth before her Sister Q. Mary

These two woodcuts, taken from a series of seventeenth-century illustrations *Popish Plots and Treasons* by Cornelius Danckerts, show Elizabeth imprisoned in the Tower, and pleading with her sister – though Elizabeth was not permitted to see Mary at this time. The figure peering through the curtains may possibly be the Lord Chancellor, Stephen Gardiner.

hostile move, and by the end of April had convinced Mary that there was no case for extreme action. A frustrated Renard reported that by English law no evidence had emerged which could convict Elizabeth, a position which was not strictly accurate, but reflected the outcome of the battle in Council. On 22 May she was removed into house arrest at Woodstock. With the benefit of hindsight, it is clear that the immediate danger was then past, but neither Elizabeth nor her worried servants knew that.

Her situation was probably not helped by the warm reception which she received on the way to Woodstock from crowds of bystanders. Her escort, Sir Henry Bedingfield, was sufficiently worried to report to the Council on a daily basis, but there was no attack on his men. Elizabeth was to spend almost a year at Woodstock, at her own expense, and closely guarded by the officious Bedingfield. Foxe makes him appear something of a buffoon, and clearly the Princess amused herself by running intellectual rings round him, which was not difficult. However, he appears to have been simply a conscientious and efficient officer, if not very bright, and if Foxe is right about the covert attempts which Gardiner made to have her assassinated, he effectively protected her. This was a less traumatic confinement than that which she had endured in the Tower, but it was a sore trial of her patience, to say nothing of her acting ability.

At last, on 17 April 1555 she was summoned back to court. This was not release but a transfer, designed to keep her under close surveillance during the critical time of the Queen's lying-in. How Elizabeth reacted to this stressful anti-climax of her sister's life, we do not know. We do not even know how much, if any, time they spent together. The Princess would have known perfectly well that if Mary should be safely delivered of a healthy child, then her own prospects of succession would recede into the hypothetical. By the same token, if neither Mary nor her child survived the ordeal, she would be Queen, unless Philip had the will and the means to prevent her. Mary, of course, knew the same, and the knowledge is unlikely to have eased relations between them.

4 *Elizabeth in danger*

A two-page letter from Elizabeth to Mary, written at about noon on 17 March 1554, at the court at Westminster where Elizabeth had been confined for about a month. It is written in the Princess' own hand, and seems to have been entirely of her own composition, including the lines she carefully drew at the end of the letter to prevent unauthorized additions. The original is damaged and the text below is supplemented from a later transcript held in the British Library.

Elizabeth had been arrested in February following first a conspiracy and then a rebellion in which Sir Thomas Wyatt led three thousand Kentish-men to the gates of London. Although the declared aim of the rebels was simply to stop Mary's marriage to Philip of Spain, its real purpose was probably to displace Mary in favour of Elizabeth. When no conclusive evidence of Elizabeth's involvement had been obtained over a month after her arrest, it was decided to send her to the more intimidating environment of the Tower of London.

Elizabeth wrote this letter in the hope that the delay it would cause would encourage Mary to re-think her decision to send her to the Tower. The twenty-year-old Princess is clearly determined to maintain that she is the Queen's 'most faithful subject' and has done absolutely no wrong. She pleads that she should be allowed to see Mary to clear her name and deny in person the false reports that the Queen has been persuaded to believe about her sister; in an interesting comparison she suggests that Thomas Seymour may have survived if he had only had the chance to talk to his brother, the Lord Protector. However, Mary did not respond to the letter, and Elizabeth was indeed sent to the Tower just the following day.

ELIZABETH WROTE:

If any ever did try this old saying – that a King's word was more than another man's oath – I most humbly beseech your majesty to verify it in me, and to remember your last promise and my last demand: that I be not condemned without answer and due proof. Which it seems that now I am, for that, without cause proved, I am by your Council from you commanded to go unto the Tower, a place more wonted [appropriate] for a false traitor than a true subject. Which though I know that I deserve it not, yet in the face of all this realm appears that it is proved. Which I pray God I may die the shamefullest death that ever any died before I may mean any such thing. And to this present hour I profess before God (who shall judge my truth, whatsoever malice shall devise) that I never practised, counselled nor consented to anything that might be prejudicial to your person any way or dangerous to the state by any mean. And therefore I humbly beseech your majesty to let me answer before yourself and not suffer me to trust your councillors – yes, and that before I go to the Tower (if it be possible); if not, before I be further condemned. Howbeit [Nevertheless] I trust assuredly your highness will give me leave to do it before I go, for that thus shamefully I may not be cried out on as now I shall be – yes and without cause. Let conscience move your highness to take some better way with me than to make me be condemned in all men's sight before my desert known.

Also I most humbly beseech your highness to pardon this my boldness, which innocency procures me to do, together with hope of your natural kindness, which I trust will not see me cast away without desert. Which what it is, I would desire no more of God but that you truly knew. Which thing I think and believe you shall never by report know unless by yourself you hear. I have heard in my time of many cast away for want of coming to the presence of their prince, and in late days I heard my lord of Somerset say that if his brother [Thomas Seymour] had been suffered to speak with him, he had never suffered. But the persuasions were made to him so great that he was brought in belief that he could not live safely if the Admiral lived, and that made him give his consent to his death. Though these persons are not to be compared to your majesty, yet I pray God as evil persuasions persuade not one sister against the other, and all for that they have heard false report and not harken [listen] to the truth

The letter continues:

known. Therefore once again, with humbleness of my heart because I am not suffered to bow the knees of my body, I humbly crave to speak with your highness. Which I would not be so bold as to desire if I knew not myself most clear, as I know myself most true. And as for the traitor [Thomas] Wyatt, he might peradventure [perhaps] write me a letter, but on my faith I never received any from him. And as for the copy of my letter sent to the French king, I pray God confound me eternally if ever I sent him word, message, token or letter by any means, and to this my truth I will stand in to my death.

I humbly crave but only one word of answer from yourself

Your highness' most faithful subject that has been from the beginning and will be to mine end,

Elizabeth.

If any euer did try this olde saynge that a kinges Worde was more than
a nother mans othe I most humbly beseche your M. to verefie it in
me and to remember your last promis and my last demaunde that I
be not codemned without answer and due profe wiche it semes that now I am for
that without cause proued I am by your counsel frome you comanded
to go vnto the tower a place more wonted for a false traitor, than a tru
subiett wiche thogh I knowe I deserue it not, yet in the face of
al this realme apperes that it is proued wiche I pray god I may dye
the shamefullist dethe that euer any died afore I may mene any suche
thinge and to this present hower I protest afor God (who shal iuge
my trueth) whatsoeuer malice shal deuis) that I neuer practised
conciled nor consented to any thinge that mighte be preiudicial
to your parson any way or dangerous to the state by any
mene and therfor I humbly beseche your maiestie to let
me answer afore your selfe and not suffer me to trust your
counselors yea and that afore I go to the tower (if it
be posible) if not afor I be further codemned howbeit I
trust assuredly your highnes wyl giue me lene to do it afor
I go for that thus shafully I may not be cried out on as now I shal
be yea and without cause let cosciens moue your highnes to
take some better way with me than to make me be condemned
in al mens sighth afor my desert knowen Also I most humbly
beseche your highnes to pardon this my boldnes wiche
innocecy procures me to do togither with hope of your natural
kindnis wiche I trust wyl not se me cast away without deserte
Wiche what it is I wold desier no more of God but that you
truly knewe. Wiche thinge I thinke and beleue you shal
neuer by report knowe vnles by your selfe you hire I haue
harde in my time of many cast away for want of cominge
to the presence of ther prince and in late days I harde my
lorde of Somerset say that if his brother had bine suffered
to speke with him he had neuer suffered but the
perswasions wer made to him so gret that he was brogth
in belefe that he coulde not liue safely if the admiral liued
and that made him giue his consent to his dethe thogh
thes parsons ar not to be copared to your maiestie yet I
pray god as iuel perswatios persuade not one sistar agaynst
the other and al for that thei haue harde false report and
not harkene to the truthe

In the event, neither situation arose. The pregnancy, if such it was, faded out amid mutterings of deceit and even witchcraft. Mary was left physically and emotionally traumatized; either her desperate longings had betrayed her, or she was seriously ill. As Philip prepared to go about his father's business, Elizabeth was allowed quietly to withdraw to her estates. Her position had been greatly strengthened by the Queen's misfortune, although nobody ventured to say so at the time. No one, apart from Mary herself, now believed that she would have a child, and although there were still extreme Catholics who talked of excluding the Princess by statute, there was no serious chance of that happening. It was no longer a question of if, but when, she would succeed her ailing sister.

Philip came to terms with reality. Unless he was prepared to fight a civil war in England, Elizabeth would in due course come to the throne; it was better to come to terms with this tough and clever young lady than to make an enemy of her. Consequently, when another crisis arose early in 1556, the King protected her. This was the so-called Dudley conspiracy, a plot by English exiles in France to invade the country and link up with a rising in the West Country; inevitably the overthrow of Mary in Elizabeth's favour was the objective. This time the Council simply notified the Princess that her name was being taken in vain, and no assumptions were made about her own involvement. Philip's instructions were apparently responsible for this caution. However, several of her most confidential servants, including Catherine Ashley and her cofferer Thomas Parry, were rounded up, interrogated, and removed from their positions. Elizabeth found herself with a new team of officers, led by Sir Thomas Pope, who were definitely not to her liking. This time, however, her protests were low key.

During 1557 Philip returned for about three months, and Elizabeth was briefly at court, but generally it was a period of withdrawal and waiting. Mary was not obviously ill, but after her husband's departure she was under the weather, and lacking in energy. By the following summer she clearly was unwell, and Philip took the precaution of sending the Count of Feria to consult with Elizabeth, to their mutual satisfaction. By October the Queen was dangerously ill, and Elizabeth quietly began to make her dispositions; a 'shadow Council' assembled at Hatfield, and her affinity (now very large) was placed on stand-by. Feria returned, and found the Princess supremely confident, and not at all disposed to be amenable to his master's purposes. On 10 November, about a week before she died, Mary recognized her sister as her heir; it was probably the bitterest surrender of her life, but it protected the lawful order, and probably saved the country from civil strife.

The one remaining wing of the Old Palace, Hatfield House. Elizabeth spent much of her childhood at Hatfield, and it was here that she was told of Mary's death in November 1558.

To Play the Queen

MONARCHY AND MATRIMONY

When Elizabeth came to the throne, a few weeks past her twenty-fifth birthday, she was a good looking and fearsomely intelligent young woman. She was also skilled and toughened in the ways of the world, and extremely self-aware. In the adverse circumstances of her sister's reign she had learned caution, patience and dissimulation. The instinct for role-play, which she had inherited from her mother, had been honed to a fine art. For five years she had played the innocent and put-upon victim; now she had to play the Queen, and to decide how to play it. Read Elizabeth's first speech as Queen; document 5, *A declaration of intent*.

By this time, Elizabeth had undergone two of the three great formative experiences of her life. She had been made particularly aware her own sexuality: how vulnerable it could make her, and yet what power it could confer if used appropriately. Over the next forty-five years, crises and problems would come and go, but the problem of juggling and balancing incompatible gender roles was a constant feature throughout. Elizabeth never for a moment forgot that she was the monarch. Unlike her sister, she never accepted that some aspects of government were inappropriate for a woman even if the traditional imagery of monarchy was exclusively masculine. The team which she had to lead and control consisted entirely of men, because no public office was open to a woman, except the Crown itself. The problem of management style was consequently with her throughout her reign. Elizabeth had no intention of being sidelined or taken for granted by men who would assume that she

This portrait shows Elizabeth in her coronation robes, which were trimmed with ermine and adorned with Tudor roses; wearing the crown and holding the orb and sceptre. She is wearing her hair loose, as was traditional at the coronation of a queen, though it has been suggested it is also a symbol of her virginity. Artist unknown.

5 A declaration of intent

Queen Elizabeth's first speech, delivered at Hatfield on 20 November 1558, just a few days after Mary's death. It is likely that Elizabeth did not prepare a written draft beforehand, but spoke spontaneously. We do not know who recorded the speech, but it would have been written down from memory afterwards and, as a result, some words or phrasing may have altered slightly. However, the substance of the speech is all Elizabeth's own, and is an early example of the political skill that she was to display throughout her reign.

As soon as Mary died, her Council would have been bound to wait on the new Queen, so this speech would have been addressed to both incoming and outgoing Councillors, as well as to any other peers who may have taken the precaution of coming to profess their allegiance. The first to be addressed is the new Secretary of State William Cecil, an astute politician who had adopted Catholicism during Mary's reign but had also entered into correspondence with Elizabeth before she came to the throne. Cecil became the new Queen's most trusted adviser, serving Elizabeth for the next forty years.

This speech contains Elizabeth's first recorded use of the metaphor of the 'two bodies' – the 'body natural' and the 'body politic', in other words the ruler as a person and the ruler as a monarch. Elizabeth used this metaphor frequently for obvious reasons; it was particularly appropriate for the Queen who identified herself, and her virginity, so closely with the State.

ELIZABETH'S SPEECH:

Words spoken by her majesty to Mr.[Sir William] Cecil:

I give you this charge, that you shall be of my Privy Council and content yourself to take pains for me and my realm. This judgement I have of you that you will not be corrupted by any manner of gift, and that you will be faithful to the state, and that without respect of my private will, you will give me that counsel that you think best, and if you shall know anything necessary to be declared to me of secrecy, you shall show it to myself only. And assure yourself I will not fail to keep taciturnity therein, and therefore herewith I charge you.

Words spoken by the Queen to the lords:

My lords, the law of nature moves me to sorrow for my sister; the burden that is fallen upon me makes me amazed, and yet, considering I am God's creature, ordained to obey His appointment, I will thereto yield, desiring from the bottom of my heart that I may have assistance of His grace to be the minister of His heavenly will in this office now committed to me. And as I am but one body naturally considered, though by His permission a body politic to govern, so I shall desire you all, my lords (chiefly you of the nobility, every one in his degree and power), to be assistant to me, that I with my ruling and you with your service may make a good account to Almighty God and leave some comfort to our posterity on earth. I mean to direct all my actions by good advice and counsel. And therefore considering that divers of you be of the ancient nobility, having your beginnings and estates of my progenitors, kings of this realm, and thereby ought in honour to have the more natural care for the maintaining of my estate and this commonwealth; some others have been of long experience in government and enabled by my father of noble memory, my brother and my late sister to bear office; the rest of you being upon special trust lately called to her service only and trust, for your service considered and rewarded; my meaning is to require of you all nothing more but faithful hearts in such service as from time to time shall be in your powers towards the preservation of me and this commonwealth. And for counsel and advice I shall accept you of my nobility, and such other of you the rest as in consultation I shall think meet and shortly appoint, to the which also, with their advice, I will join to their aid, and for ease of their burden, others meet for my service. And they which I shall not appoint, let them not think the same for any disability in them, but for that I do consider a multitude does make rather discord and confusion than good counsel. And of my goodwill you shall not doubt, using yourselves as appertains to good and loving subjects.

wordes spoken by her ma^{tie}
to m^r Cecille

20 li.

I gibe you this chardge that you shalbe of my privy counsell and content yor selfe
to take paynes for me and my realme, This iudgement I habe of you that you
will not bee corrupted wth any maner of gift, and that you wilbee faithfull to the
state, and that w^{th}out respect of my private will you will gibe me that counsaill that
you thinke best, And if you shall knowe any thinge necessarye to bee declared to me of
secretye, you shall shewe it to my selfe only, and assure yor selfe I will not fayle to keepe
taciturnitye therin, and therfore herewith I chardge you.

wordes spoken by the Queene
to the lordes.

My lordes the lawe of nature mobeth mee to sorrowe for my sister, the burthen that is
fallen uppon me maketh me amazed, And yet consideringe I am Godes creature ordeyned
to obey his appoyntment I will therto yelde, desiringe from the bottome of my harte that
I may habe assistance of his grace to bee the minister of his heabenly will in this office
nowe committed to me, And as I am but one bodye naturallye considered thoughe by his
permission a bodye politique to goberne, So I shall desire you all my lordes (cheifly you of
the nobility) every one in his degree and power to bee assistant to me; that I wth my
rulinge and you wth yor serbice may make a good accompt to Almighty God, and leabe
some comforte to our posterytye in earth, I meane to direct all my acions by good
adbise and counsell, And therfore consideringe that diberse of you bee of the auncient
Nobility, habing yor begynninges and estates of my progenitors kinges of this realme, and therby
ought in honour to habe the more naturall care for maynteyninge of my estate and
this comon wealth, Some others habe been of long experience in goberneme^{nt} and
enhabled by my father of Noble memory, my Brother and my late syster to beare
this, the rest of you beeing uppon speciall trust lately called to her serbice only
and trust for yor serbice I consydered and rewarded, my meaninge is to require of you all
nothinge more but faithfull hartes in such serbice as from tyme to tyme shalbe in yor
powers towardes the preserbacion of me and this comon wealth, And for counsell
and adbise I shall accepte you of my Nobility and such others of you the rest as in
consultacion I shall thinke meete and shortly appoynt, To the wch also wth theire adbise I
will ioyne to their ayde and for ease of their burthen others meete for my serbice;
And they wch I shall not appoynt let them not thinke the same for any disabilitye in
them, but for that I do consider a multitude doth make rather discord and confusion
then good counsell, And of my good will you shall not doubt vsing yor selbes as
apperteynethe to good and lobing subiects.

was emotional and indecisive, simply because she was a woman. Her celebrated procrastination was genuine enough because she always hoped that circumstances would resolve issues for her, thus saving her both risk and expense. However, it was also a tactic designed to emphasize the essential nature of her own role. Important decisions could not be made without her participation, and by delaying and changing her mind, she made it clear who was in control. More obviously, she used gender to dictate style. It was natural enough for the court of a woman to be dominated by themes of courtly love – Castiglione had shown this in Emilia Pia, the heroine of his *Book of the Courtier*. Elizabeth loved presiding at jousts, coyly allowing champions to wear her token, and appearing in the guise of the Queen of Faerie. However, she transposed this style into her government as well, and her ministers sometimes complained that they did not know whether they were in council, or a courtly charade. There was also a perilous side to her femininity. *La belle dame sans merci* was not a comfortable person to do business with; in addition to being (when she chose) mysterious and unattainable, she could also release a formidable and unpredictable temper.

The Queen's Champion, Sir Edward Dymoke, at Elizabeth's coronation banquet. The Champion would ride in during the coronation banquet (usually in Westminster Hall) and throw down his gauntlet, challenging anyone who would oppose the new sovereign.

The quintessential stage for all this role-play was, of course, the question of marriage. It has been suggested that Elizabeth did not marry because Thomas Seymour had put her off the whole business of sex, or because she knew herself to be infertile. However, there is no evidence that she ever made a conscious decision not to wed, and each option was real as long as it lasted. It was time which

William Cecil, Lord Burghley. Secretary (1558–72), Lord Treasurer (1572–98). Elizabeth's longest serving and most influential adviser. Artist unknown.

eventually foreclosed. Unlike Mary, Elizabeth never felt the need for masculine support in the business of ruling. Emotional support she may have desired, but the real purpose of marriage was procreation – in other words, the succession. No marriage, no children: no children, no direct heir. However, by about 1580 that ceased to be a possibility. Only Elizabeth herself knew exactly when, but the Anjou negotiation which collapsed in 1581 was the last. She was berated both at the time and afterwards for irresponsibility, but the equation was a complex one.

In favour of marriage was the possibility of an heir, and of a stable and supportive foreign alliance. Against were the dangers of choosing the wrong man, of foreign interference in English affairs and, above all, of losing control, both of her government and of her own body. It is this last element which is so imponderable, because it barely features in the written records. Elizabeth did not wish to discuss it, and no one else was qualified to, but Mary had conspicuously failed to reconcile the roles of independent sovereign and dutiful wife, and her sister had witnessed this at close quarters. It was no use assuming that she could change the contemporary rules of matrimony, even if she was the Queen. It was one thing to have flattering courtly lovers dancing attendance, and quite another to be legally tied to a man who could use her as he would

any other woman. So when it came to the point, the price was always too high. That is not to say that the negotiations were not serious and sincere, but they always failed at the point of personal commitment. However clearly Elizabeth could see the advantages of any union, ultimately she would never surrender control. Read Elizabeth's response to Parliament's pressure on her to take a husband; document 6, *To marry – or not?*

6   *To marry – or not?*

Part of Elizabeth's response, of 28 January 1563, to the House of Commons petition that she should marry. This is a two-page draft copied down by a secretary.

Elizabeth's marriage had been a subject of intense speculation and political activity from the moment of her accession. By the time that this speech was made she had rejected the overtures of Philip II, and decided, after a great emotional crisis, not to marry Lord Robert Dudley. Negotiations for both Swedish and Habsburg marriages were going on at the time, but inconclusively. The Queen is here acknowledging the validity of the petition, but using the conflicting pressures of political and personal factors to evade giving an answer.

Petitions of this kind were to recur regularly over the next decade, from both the Lords and the Commons, because not only was Parliament worried about the succession, but its (male) members would have felt more at ease with a king in place – even if he had to be a foreigner. Elizabeth, it was beginning to transpire, was extremely reluctant to surrender any part of the control which she presently possessed, both over her person and her kingdom. However, at the time of this speech she was still only twenty-nine and had not yet made any final decision about marriage.

ELIZABETH'S RESPONSE:

1563 The Speaker of your Parliament

Williams [Thomas Williams, Speaker] I have heard by you the common request of my Commons, which I may well term (methinks) the whole realm because they give, as I have heard, in all these matters of parliament their common consent to such as be here assembled. The weight and greatness of this matter might cause in me, being a woman wanting both wit and memory, some fear to speak and bashfulness besides, a thing appropriate to my sex. But yet the princely seat and kingly throne wherein God (though unworthy) has constituted men, makes these two causes to seem little in mine eyes, though grievous perhaps to your ears, and emboldens me to say somewhat in this matter, which I mean only to touch but not presently to answer. For this so great a demand needs both great and grave advice. I read of a philosopher whose deeds upon this occasion I remember better than his name who always when he was required to give answer in any hard question of school points would rehearse over his alphabet before he would proceed to any further answer therein, not for that he could not presently have answered, but have his wits the riper and better sharpened to answer the matter withal. If he, a common man, but in matters of school took such delay the better to show his eloquent tale, great cause may justly move me in this, so great a matter touching the benefits of this realm and the safety of you all, to defer mine answer to another time, wherein I assure you the consideration of mine own safety (although I thank you for the great care that you seem to have thereof) shall be little in comparison of that great regard that I mean to have of the safety and surety of you all. And although God of late seemed to touch me rather like one that He chastised [she had suffered a dangerous attack of smallpox in September 1562] than one that He punished, and although death possessed almost every joint of me, so as I wished then that the feeble thread of life, which lasted (methought) all too long, might by Clotho's hand [one of the Fates] have quietly been cut off, yet desired I not then life (as I have some witnesses here) so much for mine own safety as for yours. For I know that in exchanging of this reign I should have enjoyed a better reign where residence is perpetual …

The response continues:

…Lastly, because I will discharge some restless heads in whose brains the needless hammers beat with vain judgement that I should mislike this their petition, I say that of the matter and sum thereof I like and allow very well. As to the circumstances, if any be, I mean upon further advice further to answer. And so I assure you all that though after my death you may have many stepdames, yet shall you never have any more [natural] mother than I mean to be unto you all.

1563

Williams. I have heard by you the Common Request
of my Commons, which I may well term (me thinketh) the
whole Realm, because they give, as I have heard in all
there Matters of Parliamt. their common consent to such as
be here assembled. The weight, and greatnes of this
Matter might cause in me being a Woman wanting both
witt, and memory some feare to speake, and bashfulnes
besides, a thing appropriat to my Sex. But yet the
princely Seat, and Kingly Throne, wherein God (though
unworthy) hath constituted me, maketh these two causes
to seeme little in mine eyes, though grievous perhaps to
your eares, and boldeneth me to say some what in this Matter,
which I mean onely to touche, but not greatly to answer:
for this so great a demand needeth both great, and grave
advise. I read of a Philosopher, whose deedes upon this
occasion I remember better, than his name, who al-
wayes, when he was required to give answer in any hard
question of School-Points, would rehearse over his Alphabet, before he would proceed to any further answer therein
not for that he could not presently have answered, but
have his witts the riper, and better sharpened to answer
the Matter withall. If he a common Man, but in matters of Schoole took such delay, the better to shew his
eloquent tale; great cause may justly move me in this
so great a Matter touching ye benefit of this Realm, and the safety
of you all to differ mine Answer till some other time,
wherein I assure you the consideration of my own safety
(although I thanke you for the great care, that you seem to
have thereof) shall bee little in comparison of that great
regard, that I mean to have of the safety, and surety of you all.
And though God of late seemed to touch me, rather like one
that he chastised, than one that He punished, and though Death
possessed almost every joynt of me, so as I wished then that
the feeble thread of Life, which lasted (me thought) all too
long, might by Clotho's hand have quietly been cutt off:
Yet desired I not then life (as I have some witnesses here) so
much for mine own safety, as for yours: For I knew that in
exchanging of this Reign, I should have enjoyed a better Reign,
where Residence is perpetuall. There needs no boding of
my band. I know now as well, as I did before, that I am
                                                        mortal

Robert Dudley, Earl of Leicester, attributed to Steven van der Meulen. Leicester was the Queen's principal favourite and the affectionate friendship between them endured for over thirty years. His 'last letter' to Elizabeth (see document 7, *A sad farewell*) is testimony to this unique relationship.

The Queen was bombarded with offers of marriage, but only three, or perhaps four, were taken seriously over any length of time. The first, and by far the most significant from Elizabeth's point of view, was not exactly an offer, but it was certainly an opportunity. She had known Robert Dudley since they were both children, and had kept in touch with him during the dark days of Mary's reign. When she came to the throne, she made her friend Master of the Horse, and it was generally noted that she favoured him. However, during the course of 1559 friendship became love. Dudley was not her equal as an intellectual, but he was a lively conversationalist and a gifted courtier. He was also dashing and handsome, and had much the same kind of sex-appeal as Thomas Seymour. Intentionally or otherwise he stimulated a sharp attack of old-fashioned lust in Elizabeth; they took to meeting at indiscreet hours of the day and night, and rumours quickly spread that they were sleeping together. These rumours were almost certainly untrue. The fact that Dudley had a wife was relevant, if not necessarily decisive, but Elizabeth, for all her infatuation, had far too much to lose. Their relationship created a furore. Lord Robert was unpopular, and a political maverick; more importantly, his pretensions were opposed by the adviser upon whom the Queen most depended, and whom she most trusted, William Cecil. Foreign courts sniggered, and English diplomats hung their heads in shame.

Then in September 1560 Amy Dudley died, almost certainly of natural causes but in suspicious circumstances. The scandal was immense, and Elizabeth did not know whether to be exhilarated or devastated. Her struggle between desire and duty was traumatic and lasted for many months, but in the event her instincts for political survival prevailed. Lord Robert was created Earl of Leicester and became a member of the Privy Council, and as such was a major political figure for the rest of his life. His relationship with the Queen continued to be unique, but was no longer in any danger of becoming physical. There is no reason to suppose that this experience caused Elizabeth to forswear marriage as a political option, but it taught her a lesson of deep significance: never take any major decision for emotional reasons alone.

It should not be supposed, however, that it was only calculating prudence which prompted this renunciation. Elizabeth was a young woman of deep piety, and took her chastity seriously. Even if she could have avoided the obvious risks, she would not have slept with any man outside the context of marriage. The fact that she had a lively and at times overpowering sexuality made for intense difficulties, and helps to explain her apparently irrational hatred of marriage among her female servants, and her fits of violent ill-humour. Her Privy Chamber was her retreat from the pervasive world of men and their insensitive priorities. The marriage of any member represented an intrusion, a division of loyalty and love which she found hard to accept. However, her outbursts were not consistent, and her hostility usually ephemeral.

7 *A sad farewell*

A letter from Robert Dudley, Earl of Leicester to the Queen, 29 August 1588.

Leicester remained a favourite of Elizabeth for over thirty years despite his secret marriage to the widow of Walter Devereux, Earl of Essex, in 1578, and his disastrous expedition to aid the Dutch in their revolt against Spain in 1585. This routine note is significant because it was the last communication between the old friends: Leicester died on 4 September at his house in Cornbury in Oxfordshire. There were rumours that he died of poison intended for his wife, but his death was not sudden; as the letter reveals, he was already ill (although the exact nature of his illness is unknown) and Elizabeth had given him permission to take the waters at Buxton (he refers to 'hoping to find perfect cure at the bath'). Elizabeth, who was then in her mid-fifties, seems to have been unwell herself around this time.

When the note was written, Leicester was staying at Rycote in Oxfordshire, with Lady Norris, a former servant of Elizabeth's and the mother of Sir John Norris. Elizabeth was a regular visitor to Rycote, though it had never been part of her estate.

There is no record of what the 'token' from Elizabeth to Leicester was, although a token was usually a ring or a type of trinket; 'young Tracey' was the servant who delivered it.

It is perhaps revealing that Elizabeth kept this little note, endorsed 'his last letter', among her personal possessions for the remaining fifteen years of her life.

LEICESTER WROTE:

I most humbly beseech your Majesty to pardon your poor old servant to be thus bold in sending to know how my gracious lady does, and what ease of her late pain she finds, being the chiefest thing in the world that I do pray for, for her to have good health and long life. For my own poor case I continue still your medicine and find it amends much better than any other thing that hath been given me. Thus hoping to find perfect cure at the bath, with the continuance of my wonted [usual] prayer for your Majesty's most happy preservation, I humbly kiss your foot. From your old lodging at Rycote this Thursday morning, ready to take on my journey,

by your Majesty's most faithful and obedient servant,

R. Leicester

Even as I had written thus much, I received your Majesty's token by young Tracey.

I most humbly beseech your Majesty to pardon this poor
old man to be thus bold in sending to know how your
gracious Majesty doth, and what ease of your late pains you
finde, being the chiefest thing in this world I do
pray for & for her to have good health and long life,
for my own poor case, I continue still yt medicine
and finde yt amend much better than any other
thing yt hath given me. That I might so
finde perfect cure of my ease, at the continuance
of my ... prayer for yt most most gracious
... I humbly ... my ... this
old lodging at ... this thursday morning
ready to take on my Journey

by yr Majtys most faithful and
obedient servant

R. Leycester

even as I did write this
... I now ... by
...

148

(55)

SUPREME GOVERNOR

More significant than the effect on her private life, Elizabeth's piety prompted her to take her public religious responsibilities with great seriousness. This is reflected in the speech she gave to her bishops in 1585, summarized in document 8, *Elizabeth and the Church*. No one doubted that her conformity in 1553 had been constrained, and even the most earnest of her Godly subjects never reproached her with it. But the weight of expectation when she came to the throne was very great. What most of her subjects were looking for was a return to English priorities. They wanted to escape from Spanish influence, and were prepared to accept another repudiation of the Pope. Elizabeth never had any intention of stopping at that, however strongly she was advised to do so. Her purpose, and indeed her duty as she saw it, was to establish a Church which satisfied her own conscience, and then to make it as acceptable as possible to as many of her subjects as possible.

What was established in the parliament of 1559 was an uncompromisingly Protestant Church, reformed in doctrine and worship, conservative only in form. In fact, it was a return to her brother's settlement, and it represented the Queen's considered position. She defended it thereafter with great tenacity and consistency, because it was the will of God that she should be Supreme Governor, and it was her duty to serve God in accordance with her own conscience. It was up to her to decide which compromises to make, and which not to make, in enforcing this settlement. She was willing to listen to advice, but refused to be hectored or bullied into making changes that she did not want.

The Catholic opposition eventually defined its own position. After more than a decade during which the Queen had consistently attempted to accommodate as many conservatives as possible, there was rebellion in the north of England, and the Pope declared Elizabeth deposed. These two events handed the initiative to the Queen; thereafter to be loyal to the Crown and a good Englishman

The frontispiece of Elizabeth's personal prayer book, showing Elizabeth at prayer (1569).

Elizabeth Regina.

2. PARALIPOM. 6.

Domine Deus Israel, non est similis tui Deus in cœlo & in terra, qui pacta custodis & misericordiam cum seruis tuis, qui ambulant coram te in toto corde suo.

Elizabeth and the Church

Extracts from the clerk's two-page summary of Elizabeth's speech to her bishops and other clergy at Somerset Place, 27 February 1585.

The context of this meeting is clear from the text. Clerical subsidies were voted separately, and by the Convocations, not by Parliament. There were two Convocations, one for Canterbury Province and the other for York: Canterbury was much the larger and more important. By 1585 the Convocations had lost most of their earlier power and functions to the Parliament, which legislated on all matters to do with regulating the national Church. Convocations met at the same time as Parliaments, and the lay and clerical subsidies were part of the same taxation package. The tension between the lay Councillors, and particularly Cecil, on the one hand, and the Archbishop, John Whitgift, on the other comes through clearly. Elizabeth is emphasizing her own control rather than taking sides.

The issue about unfit clergy was a long-running one, because ordinations had declined steeply after 1558, and there was an acute shortage, particularly of preachers, which the Queen was reluctant to acknowledge. By the end of the century the situation was improving rapidly, as graduates came forward in increasing numbers.

ELIZABETH'S SPEECH TO HER BISHOPS:

A brief effect of her Majesty's speech unto the bishops and other of the clergy offering unto her their subsidy in her Privy Chamber at Somerset Place, 27 February 1584 [5] at what time there were of the clergy my lord Archbishop of Canterbury [John Whitgift], the bishops of Worcester, Sarum and Rochester, Mr. Archdeacon of Canterbury prolocutor [Speaker of the Lower House of Convocation], the Deans of Pauls, Westminster and Ely, Doctor Bell and Doctor Bound, and in the presence of my lords Chancellor, Treasurer, Leicester, Bedford, Chamberlain and Hampton, Mr. Secretary Walsingham and Mr. Solicitor.

1. Imprimis. [First (in a list of items)] The subsidy being delivered by the Archbishop of Canterbury in the name of the whole clergy, her majesty answered that she did accept of it thankfully, and the rather for that it came voluntarily and frankly, whereas the laity must be entreated and moved thereunto. My lord Treasurer [Lord Burghley], standing by, said Madame, these men come with mites [small coins], but we will come with pounds.

Her majesty answered, I esteem more of their mites than of your pounds, for that they come of themselves not moved, but you tarry [wait] till you be urged thereunto, and gave the clergy thanks, saying, Whatsoever you have bestowed upon me, I am to bestow it upon you again. God grant I may bestow it to His glory and the benefit of this realm.

2. Then she said unto the bishop, We understand that some of the Nether House [the Commons] have used divers reproachful speeches against you tending greatly to your dishonour, which we will not suffer; and that they meddle with matters above their capacity not appertaining unto them, for the which we will call some of them to an account. And we understand they be countenanced by some of our Council, which we will redress or else uncouncil some of them. But, said she, we will not charge the whole House with this disorder, for although there be some intemperate and rash heads in that House, yet there be many wise and discreet men who do find just cause of grievance against some of you; first in that you have not greater care in making ministers, whereof some be of such lewd [disorderly] life and corrupt behaviour whereof we know of some such that be not worthy to come into any honest company.......

5. After this, she wished the bishops to look unto private conventicles [secret religious meetings]. And now, quod [said] she, I miss my Lord of London, who looks no better unto the city, where every merchant must have his schoolmaster and nightly conventicles expounding scripture and catechizing their servants and maids, in so much that I have heard how some of their maids have not sticked [hesitated] to control learned preachers, and to say that such a man taught otherwise in our house.......

7. Then spoke my Lord of Canterbury, saying, Madame for mine own part, I will look unto these things as well as I can, and I will take such order with my brethren as I trust they will look better unto such things. But, Madam, let me use the best means I can, some things will escape and be amiss; and when it is so, I would every man were charged with his own fault and not the fault of one or two to be laid unto all.

8. Then spake my Lord Treasurer, saying, Truly, my lord, her majesty has declared unto you a marvellous great fault in that you make in this time of light so many lewd [ignorant] and unlearned ministers.

My Lord of Canterbury said, Well.

Quod her Majesty, Draw articles and charge them with it that have offended.

I do not burden, quod my Lord Treasurer, them that be here, but it is the Bishop of Lichfield and Coventry [William Overton] that I mean, who made seventy ministers in one day for money; some tailors, some shoemakers, and other crass men. I am sure the greatest part of them is not worthy to keep horses ...

10. Then said my Lord of Canterbury, We complain, in these days, of darkness in time of light, of ignorance in time of learning, of want of preachers in time of plenty. I dare avouch, let all records be sought, and there was never that number of learned preachers that is in these days, and do and will increase daily more and more.....

68 215

(68.)

required subscription to the Acts of Settlement and the Thirty-Nine Articles. Conservatism (which no longer meant Catholic loyalties) became a matter of taste, and Catholic recusancy potential treason. In view of the papal pronouncement, Elizabeth had little option but to treat priests as traitors, and the Catholic threat swiftly became subsumed in the general foreign threat represented by the war with Spain. This, more than anything else, pushed the Queen and her subjects together, and gave her that demonstrative popularity which she found so enjoyable and gratifying. The fact that there were numerous plots against the Queen's life may have raised anxiety levels, but it did wonders for the solidarity of the regime.

John Whitgift, Archbishop of Canterbury (seventeenth-century engraving, after George Virtue).

In this respect, agitations from within the Godly camp were much more troublesome. These came from men who, while they accepted Elizabeth as a Godly Prince, believed that she had left the Reformation incomplete. For about twenty-five years they made a perpetual nuisance of themselves, in Parliament, in Convocation, and in the country at large. Elizabeth listened with varying degrees of impatience, and rejected virtually all their demands. This was partly because such moves would have undermined the consensus which she was striving to achieve, but more because they did not appeal to her own sense of the Divine order. How dare they try to tell her how to run the Church, when God had entrusted that duty to her!

Having secured quite a lot of powerful backing, both in the Council and in Parliament, these puritan agitators eventually shot themselves in the foot. In 1588 they launched a series of mocking and scurrilous pamphlets, known as the *Marprelate Tracts*, against the authority of bishops. These immediately sounded warning bells among the lay aristocracy. Such populist attacks on one form of authority could easily spread to others: no bishops, no aristocrats. Puritan politics became unfashionable, and with several of their early leaders dead, after 1590 the survivors temporarily sank beneath the horizon. Elizabeth, in fact, was not overly fond of bishops, and even less fond of their wives, but they represented her chosen means of governing the Church, and an attack on them was consequently an attack on her. It was not until 1583 that she eventually found an Archbishop entirely to her liking in the person of John Whitgift, and he became the first (and only) prelate to join her Privy Council; a fact which is also eloquent of the jealousy with which she guarded her own ecclesiastical authority.

DEFENSIVE MANOEUVRES

Once Elizabeth's ardour for Robert Dudley had cooled, marriage became largely an issue of foreign policy. Although there were others who for a time fancied their chances, there was no other serious contender for the Queen's hand within England. At first, common sense dictated a continuation of the existing Habsburg alliance. Although that did not extend to entertaining Philip's own offer, it did lead to a serious negotiation, extending over several years, for the hand of the Archduke Charles of Austria, son of the Emperor Ferdinand, and Philip's cousin. The impossibility of religious compromise, and generally deteriorating relations with the Habsburgs ended that possibility by 1568, and it seems that Elizabeth regarded it as a purely political matter. We have no indication of her private feelings.

Overleaf: Elizabeth receiving two Dutch ambassadors, shortly before Leicester's expedition to the Low Countries, 1585. Leicester and Walsingham are also in attendance, along with Mary, Queen of Scots, who is seated on the floor in the corner.

Walbrun   Cunigam   Ambaßadur

The second major negotiation related to Henri, Duke of Anjou, the brother of the French King, and was indicative of the fact that England now regarded Spain, rather than France, as the main threat to its security. Both Charles IX and Elizabeth wanted the union for political reasons, and again private feelings don't seem to have entered the equation. Henri, however, was a *dévot*, and again the negotiation failed for religious reasons, although much of its purpose was achieved by the purely pragmatic Treaty of Blois in 1572.

The third significant negotiation concerned Henri's younger brother, François, also, confusingly, Duke of Anjou, and lasted from 1579 to 1581. This was entangled with attempts to undermine Philip's control of the Netherlands, and on the surface also appears purely political. However, this time the Queen's personal involvement was conspicuous, and is evident in the letter she wrote to François in 1579 (see document 9, *Wooing François*). She took the initiative, invited François to visit her, and sent out various signals of commitment. Her Council were confused. Whereas there had been considerable support for both Charles and Henri, there was very little support for François, and the prevailing opinion seems to have been that Elizabeth was about to make a fool of herself. Councillors expressed such views cautiously, but her subjects at large were more frank. The proposal was widely and deeply unpopular, largely because it was now believed that the Queen was past childbearing, and would be compromising herself and her realm for nothing. It was at this point that Elizabeth first became generally represented as the Virgin Queen, and it seems clear that the integrity of Elizabeth's natural body was being used as a symbol for the integrity of her realm. Faced with such powerfully expressed dissent, she backed off and accepted that marriage was no longer an option.

François, Duke of Alençon and Anjou, by François Clouet. Elizabeth affectionately nicknamed Anjou her 'frog'.

Elizabethan plan of defences around Plymouth Sound, Devon, showing soldiers firing muskets and cannons, and their range.

Every step of Elizabeth's foreign policy, with the exception of an ill-advised attempt to recover Calais in 1562 (see her letter to Philip II; document 10, *Intervention in France*), was dictated by defensive considerations. It was to prevent Scotland from being used as a base by the French that she intervened there in 1560. It was to prevent the Low Countries from being used in the same way by Spain that she held her nose and supported the rebels there. Eventually, when there appeared to be no option, she signed the Treaty of Nonsuch with the Dutch in 1585, and committed herself to a war that would last for the rest of the reign. Unlike her father, she had no ambitions either for territory or for military glory; one of the advantages of being a woman was that she could forgo the latter without losing face. Even in Ireland her main concern was not to subjugate (or civilize) the Irish, or to reward her courtiers with Irish land, although that happened; it was not even to spread the gospel, but to prevent the rebels from giving Philip a usable bridgehead.

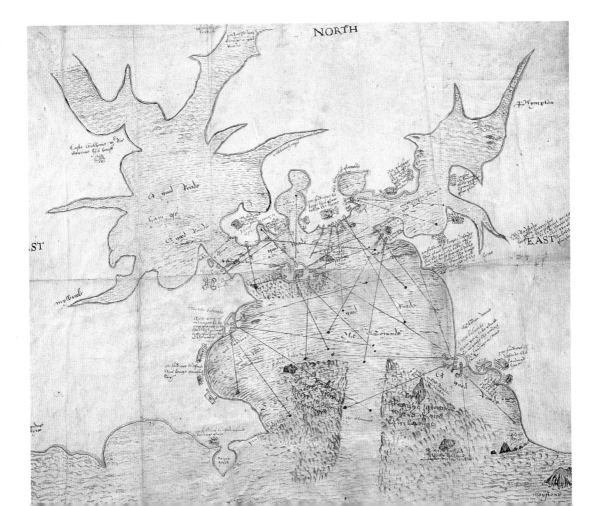

9 Wooing François

A letter from Elizabeth to François, Duke of Anjou, 19 December 1579. The original, in French, is a two-page draft in Elizabeth's own hand.

There had been a prolonged and ultimately fruitless negotiation for a marriage between Elizabeth and François between 1572 and 1578. Early in 1579, at the age of forty-five, and contrary to all expectations, the Queen herself revived the plan. Anjou, who was heir to his childless brother Henri III, was keen for a variety of reasons, not least to secure English support for his schemes in the Low Countries. In August 1579 he had visited England, and Elizabeth had given clear indications of her intention to marry him.

This letter was written a month after a treaty providing for marriage had been authorized, and it shows clear signs of personal affection. However, by the end of January 1580 the Queen had yielded to those opposed to the match, and informed Anjou that there was no prospect of their union in the present political and religious climate.

The 'thing long awaited' referred to at the start of the letter appears to have been some news of the settlement of France's internal problems. Sir Edward Stafford was the Queen's special envoy entrusted with the marriage negotiation, who became ambassador to France in 1583. The 'cause of the King of Navarre' was Protestantism: Henri, King of Navarre led the Protestant (Huguenot) faction. Jean de Simier, about whom Elizabeth enquires, was Anjou's representative at the English court, who had fallen foul of his master.

ELIZABETH WROTE:

My dearest, If the thing long awaited had been good when it arrived, I had been better content with the long wait which it pleased [Sir Edward] Stafford to afford me. But seeing that the peace seems only half made, I do not see too much reason for his delay, except that he makes me believe that this is done by your commandment, to whom I am entirely willing to be obedient. And having just at this turn received letters from France that the King is prolonging this peace under several difficulties which will not be possible to resolve too soon, I would be very happy if people allowed themselves to be astonished at his long stay, assuring myself that some of them are making sport of him.

And for the cause of the King of Navarre [Henri, later Henri IV] and his party, this I will make bold to tell you; that it will touch you very near in reputation if you should leave him in worse state than they were at the beginning of these new troubles. For if their greatest sureties were torn from them, how could they trust to the king in this? – adding that the King himself sent to tell me by his ambassador that he would not deny them the first pacification and would ask nothing except the cities and places newly taken. You will forgive me the curiosity that holds me to your actions, to whom I wish all the honour and glory that can accrue to the perpetual renown of a prince. I assure myself that desire of greatness after this peace will not blind your eyes so as to make you omit that which will be for the safety of those that trust in your goodness.

As for the commissioners, I believe that they will resemble words which, recited too many times, make the tongue slip out of order. I see that

The letter continues:

time runs on, and I with it, which renders me unfit to please as I would wish. And I am almost in agreement with those who do not quit reminding you of my faults. But God, I hope, will govern all for your good. Let it not displease you, Monsieur, that I ask some answer about [Jean de] Simier, for whom I wish some end to his unhappiness – either that he may be condemned justly and you purged of a crime often imputed to princes, whose favours are said to hang by very slender threads, or that he may be employed in your service to shut the mouths of scandal-mongers who do not cease passing their time on public affairs in order to make their expounding of them.

My dearest, I give you now a fair mirror to see there very clearly the foolishness of my understanding, which I once found so suited to hoping for a good conclusion, weighing the place where you reside with the company that is there. We poor inhabitants of the barbarous isle must be careful in appearing for judgement where such ingenious judges of our knowledge hold their seat in so high a place in your favour. But in making my appeal to Monsieur alone and undivided, I will not let my suit drop. And if you would have me given over to the rack, I will not put a gloss on this text, assuring myself that you understand it only too well. Finally, my soul [sic] request consists in this; that you always hold me as the same one whom you have obliged to be dedicated to you. And that I can only be she who has lodged you in the first rank of what is dearest to me, as God can best witness, to whom I will not cease my supplications that he grant you a hundred years of life. With my very humble remembrances to be commended to my dearest. From Westminster this nineteenth of December.

Your most assured, as she is obliged to be,

Elizabeth R.

Mo trescher, Si la chose longue que attendu eust bon esté
quant elle arriva Je cuisse esté mieulx satisfaicte
de la longue attente qu'il a pleu a Stafford
me prester Mais Voyant que la paix desja
que ademy faicte Je ne Voy trop de rayson qui
faicte sa demeure Sino qu'il me faict a croyre
qu'il si fust par vostre commandement a qui
J'ay tante volunté qu'il obaye. Et ayant
tout a l'heure receu lettres de france qui Le Roy
prolonge ceste paix soubz quelques difficultés
qui ne se pourrot tres tost coeurire Je serois
tresaise qu'on laissast s'esbahir de so longue
arreste m'assurant que quelque temps s'y en
sont leur remis Et pour la cause du Roy de
Navarre et sa partie Cesi Je prendray la
hardiesse de Vous dire qu'il nous touchera
bien pres en reputation que ne le laisser
en pire estat qu'ilz furent au commencement
de ces nouveaulx troubles Car si leur plus
grandes bourdis leur fussent arrachés commut
se tiroient y du Roy adioustant que le Roy
aussi me manda dire par so l'embassadeur
qu'il se reunieroit la premiere pacificatio
et ne demanderoit sino les Villes et
lieux, vous debvroient prendre Vousme si
pardonners la curiosité qui me tient au
Vos actions. A qui Je souhait tout l'honneur
et courage qui peut arriver a la perpetuelle
renommee de Prince, Je m'assure que
desir de grandeur apres ceste paix me
vous aveuglera les yeulx pour vous fayre
omettre ce qui sera pour le bien de ceulx
qui se fient en Vostre costé. Quant aux
commissaires Je croy qu'ilz resembleront
aux motz qui trop de fois se recitant font
la langue chopper hors d'ordre Je Voy que le

Extracts from an English, five-page, draft of a letter from Elizabeth to Philip II of Spain, 30 September 1562. It represents the Queen's views but was largely composed by Cecil, and written by his secretary.

Captured by Edward III in 1346, the port of Calais had been in English hands until it was retaken by France in January 1558. Philip had then made a rather half-hearted attempt to persuade the French to give it back to the English in the Treaty of Cateau Cambrésis in 1559. In this letter, Elizabeth is seeking to persuade him that the treaty which she has just signed with the French Huguenots is simply for the recovery of Calais – an objective which she assumes he will accept as legitimate. She is aware that Philip's sympathies, which have not yet been declared, are likely to be with the Guises, who are the main objects of her own hostility. Anxious to deflect any hostile reaction from the King of Spain, she claims that she is not supporting the Protestants as such (which was not what she told her own people), and that one of her aims is to support the authority of the French Crown (which was being economical with the truth).

The English occupation of Le Havre which followed (from October 1562 to June 1563) was a disaster, partly because plague broke out in the town, and partly because the French factions resolved their differences and combined against the garrison. When France and England agreed the Treaty of Troyes in April 1564, Elizabeth was forced to finally abandon all claim to Calais.

ELIZABETH'S LETTER:

Although your ambassador here resident [Alvaro de Quadra, Bishop of Avila] with us has of late times in your name dealt with us to understand our disposition touching these troubles in France, and the rather because he perceived that we did put a number of our subjects in order of defence both for the sea and land, to whom we made such reasonable answer as ought to satisfy him; yet because we have been in mind now of a long time to impart to you our concept and judgement hereof, wherein we have been occasioned to forebear only by the mutability of the proceedings of our neighbours in France and for that also we have some cause to doubt of the manner of the report of your ambassador, having found him in his negotiations divers times to have more respect toward the weal [welfare] of others than of us and our country; we have thought not only to give special charge to our ambassador there resident [Dr. Thomas Man] with you to declare plainly and sincerely our disposition and meaning, but also by these our own letters to import what we

The letter continues:

think of these troubles in France for our particular, and secondly what we are advised upon good considerations, not doubting but, both for your sincere and brotherly friendship and for your wisdom, you will interpret and allow of our actions with such equity as the causes do require.

Surely we have been much troubled and perplexed from the beginning of these divisions in France, and upon divers causes. First because we had a great compassion to see the young king [Charles IX] our brother so abused by his subjects as his authority could not direct them to accord. Next thereto, we feared that hereof might follow an universal trouble to the rest of Christendom, considering the quarrel was discovered and published to me for the matter of religion. Lastly, which touched us most nearly and properly, we perceived that the Duke of Guise and his House was the principal head of one part, and that they daily so increased their force as in the end they became commanders of all things in France, and thereupon such manner of hostile dealing used in divers sorts against our subjects and merchants in sundry parts of France as we were constrained to look about us what peril might ensue to our own estate and country ...

... And so we mean to direct our actions as, without any injury or violence to the French king or any of his subjects, we intend to live in good peace with the said French king, and to save to our realm in this convenient time our right to Calais with surety. Which manifestly we see by their proceeding they mean not to deliver, although in very deed we can prove that they ought presently to restore it to us. And now our good brother, seeing this is our disposition and intent, wherein it may appear that we mean to do no person wrong but to provide and foresee how apparent dangers to our estate may be diverted, and that we might not remain in this kind of unsurety to have our Calais restored to us – whereof we be assured you for divers good causes will have special regard – We trust you will not only allow of our intent but also, as you may conveniently, further us as far forth as our purpose to have Calais and peace with our neighbours does extend ...

Although the embassador here resident with vs
hath of late times in the name delt with vs to
vnderstand our disposition towching these troubles in ffrance
and the rather becawse he perceaved that we did putt
a nombre of our subiects in order of defense both by
the sea and land, to whom we made such answer (resonably)
as ought to satisfie him. yet becawse we have
now of a long tyme
ben in mynd drawing all these forbears to impart
to yow our purpose and iudgment therof, wherin
we have ben occationed to forbeare only by the
mutabilitie of the procedings of our neighbours in
ffrance, and for that also we have some cawse
to dowbt of the maner of the report of the embassador
having sent him in his negociations to have more
respect towards the weale of others then of vs and
our doings: we have thought not only to
give speciall charg to our embassador there resident
with yow to declare plainely & sincerely our
disposition and meaning, but also by these
of owne to impart briefly what we

chipiona

Sta lucar de Barra meda

Rota

Xères fronter.

Portal

las pueres

Sta katarina

el puerto de Sta maria

Rio Guadelette

M

Cadiz

A. The great and first fort in cadiz
b. The Second fort
c. The Towne gate, ordnance vppon it,
d. The gallies at our comming in
E. Caruoyles and smal Barkes
F. Ships, Aragozia, Biscayns, frensh, hulkes at puental
G. Roaders at pointal
h. a Ship of the Marques of Sta crus
J. Ships and gallies by port Rial
k. gallies to haue stoyd the lions passadge that way

3 Admirals { o for the Bonauenter
              o for the Lyon
              o marchant Rial

l. the gallies dreuen back by ye Lyon
   columbe de hercules
o m. The pece that hit ye lion
o n. a pece planted for G

a. The Bonauenter
b. The Lyon
c. The marchant Rial } At ther first Ankor
A. rest of the fleete

d. the Bonauenter at her second Ankoring
e. The Bonauenter at her third Ankoring
f. The lion at second Ankoring
G. The rest of the fleet at Second Ankoring
h. the Edward Bonauenter a ground
J. the lion at Third Ankoring

M. our fleet at Anker vppon a brauude

Isla de Cadiz

Sta pedro

Puente de Suaça   20

Puerto Real

W. Borough

Scale of English myels

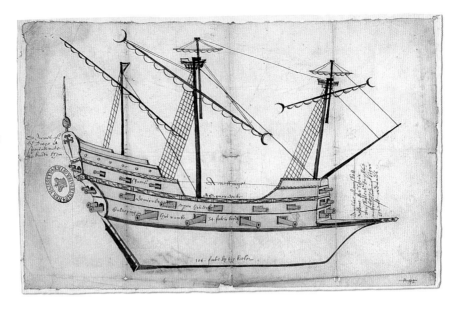

Map of the key Spanish port of Cadiz, 1587, showing the city, harbour and vicinity, with positions of English and Spanish warships. In the spring of 1587, Sir Francis Drake attacked Cadiz and burned a large proportion of the Spanish fleet, delaying the Armada by at least six months.

A Spanish galleon at the time of the Armada.

In only one respect did Elizabeth signal an aggressive strategic intention, and that was in promoting the global ambitions of her merchants and seamen. Hawkins and Drake in particular were expansionists. They were pirates as well as merchants and explorers, and the Queen supported them diplomatically and logistically, investing ships, armaments, and even money. She was far more engaged than her father or grandfather had been, and it was one of her most farsighted adventures. She did not need to build up the navy; that was already in good fettle at her accession (see document 11, *A glimpse of seapower*), but she did develop it, spend money on it, and appoint efficient men to run it. When war came, 80 per cent of it was fought at sea, and her investment was amply repaid. Tactically, the English were often aggressive, and although there were failures like the Lisbon expedition of 1589, generally they were remarkably successful. In theory there was no way in which a strained and ramshackle Anglo–Dutch alliance could have stood up to the power of Spain, but it did, and the defeat of the Armada in 1588 became not only the great symbol of God's favour, but also of the realm's inviolability associated with the Queen's virginity. Document 12, *Victory at sea*, is a first-hand account of the encounter with the Armada.

Extract from a naval survey, *The Book of Sea Causes*, conducted shortly after Elizabeth's accession, and before the end of the French war (April 1559).

Henry VIII had developed the navy as a standing force between 1510, when it had numbered six or seven ships, and 1545, when it numbered over fifty. In the latter year he had also set up a special council, called the Council for Marine Causes, to manage both the fleet and the dockyards. This council did not control military operations, but was responsible for maintenance, support, victualling and mobilization. It consisted of the Vice-Admiral (or Lieutenant), the Treasurer, Clerk, Clerk Controller, Surveyor and Master of the Ordnance. In 1550 a Surveyor General of the Victuals was added. In 1556 this council had been placed under the general supervision of the Lord Treasurer, and a budget or 'ordinary' of £14,000 a year had been set. During the reigns of Edward and Mary the fleet had been reduced somewhat – to about forty ships – but had been well maintained.

Elizabeth probably ordered this survey in order to reassure herself of the state of the navy, but also to obtain advice on the costs of mobilization, and future policy. Apart from the extracts given here, there were also lists of the existing ships and their state of repair, and a proposal to reduce the standing navy to thirty ships, which was not accepted. Seafaring, and the use of seapower, were keynote aspects of Elizabeth's government.

Sixteenth-century arithmetic was weak, possibly because of the continued use of roman numerals.

THE SURVEY:

Charges for putting the army in order:

The charges of which army, as well for the prest [advance payments] and conduct of the men, rigging, wages, victuals and provisions of all kind till the joining of the said army at a place certain, will amount by estimation to:

$$£10,512. \ 13s. \ 4d.$$

The charge of the whole army being furnished shall be:

Item the monthly charges of the foresaid army being joined and full furnished in fashion of war will be £11,363, which for five months will amount at 8s 6d wages and 12s victuals a man per mensem [every month] with 12d a ton for tonnage of the merchant ships, the sum of

$$£56,865$$

The charge in dissolving of the army:

Item at the dissolving of the army the transporting of the Queen's Majesty's ships and the merchants' to their several harbours, with the conduct of the rest of the men which are then to be discharged out of them, with other extraordinary charges, will amount by estimation to:

$$£4,000.$$

$$£71,377. \ 0s. \ 12d.$$
$$[sic] \ ....$$

Charges for
putting the Armie in
Order

The Charges of what Armie, aswell
for the prest and Conduct of men leyyeng
wayes victnalles & towarde purveous of all thinges
till the Joyning of the said Armie at a place
statute will amounte by estimacion to

Item the monthely chardge of the forsaid
Armie being formed & full furnished in a
season of warr with hey addicions where
The charge of the
sayd Armie being in
full furnishe waged & wagees & vitrolles & med & mensen wharfe
& towarde vittayle of the marchant Shipes
to the Somme of

Item at the dissolving of the Armie or
the transporting of the guarded men Shipes
and the marchantt to their whell
The charge
In dissolving of the
Armie harborowes with the conduct of the rest of & say say say d.
their men with our then to be Discharged &
out of them with other ordinary charge
will amounte by estimacion to

It is to be remembred is if this Armie shuld take effort that then a present &
Staie must be made that won of the Shipes of the staple do go furthe of &
merchandize

It is also to be remembred that when her ma will have an Armie of light
nombre to the Sees in maine as is afforsaid then of monethes salrin at the laste
must be gyven, and redie money for the doing thereof

It is further to be remembred if her grace will have a greater Armie then must
be a staie made of the hulles that passeth throughe the narrow Sees in to
Fraunce in the begynnyng of the yere

Extracts from a six-page letter from Sir William Winter to Sir Francis Walsingham, reporting the encounter with the Spanish Armada, 1 August (old reckoning) 1588.

Although the defeat of the Armada was caused at least as much by Spanish miscalculation and misfortune as by English prowess, and the English were quick to give God the credit, it was nevertheless a defining moment in the history of the country. The Spanish commander, the Duke of Medina Sidonia, was under strict orders not to deviate from his prime objective, which was to rendezvous with the Duke of Parma in order to escort his troopships for an invasion of England. He therefore fought a defensive action against the English fleet, keeping a tight formation as he came up the Channel. His attempts to communicate with Parma, however, were unsuccessful until the last minute. When he reached Calais, which was an open roadstead, he learned that the army would not be ready for six days. He had no option but to stop and wait, which gave the English the opportunity to launch the attack described here. Winter was a veteran who had been an officer of the navy since 1549.

As he suspected, the damage inflicted by the English guns was more severe than was at once apparent; and the ships which Medina Sidonia skilfully extricated were in no state to continue the fight. Winter did not know that one of the main reasons why the English suffered so little was that much of the Spanish ammunition did not fit their guns.

SIR WILLIAM WINTER WROTE:

May it please your honour upon Saturday the 27th of July our Admiral Lord Henry Seymour being with his fleet in the morning as high up as between Dungeness and Folkestone, attending the coming of the army we there spoke with divers ships that came from the West, who said they saw none of the army, which put us in hope (our victalling being within iii days of expiring) that we might bear into the Downs to see if the victuals were come, and to take in the same, and so to be in a readiness to do service, but we had not been there scarcely half an hour (the wind being at SSW) but we received a letter from the Lord Admiral [Howard of Effingham] by a pinnace [small boat] declaring unto us what we should do, and forthwith we made sail and got out, not having any time to relieve ourselves with victuals, and bare [sail] over to the French coast ... The Spanish Army was anchored to the eastward of Calais cliffs, very round and near together not far from the shore, our army not being past a mile and a half behind them ... and immediately so soon as my Lord Admiral's ship was come to an anchor, his Lordship sent his pinnace aboard [across to] my ship for me and a messenger in the same commanding me to come aboard his Lordship [his ship], which I did, and having viewed the great and hugeness of the Spanish Army and did consider that it was not possible to move them but by the device of firing of ships, which would make them to lose the only rode [anchorage] which was apt and meet for their purpose ... Upon Sunday being the 28th day my Lord put out his flag of council early, the Armies both riding still, and after the assembly of the council it was concluded that the practice for the firing of ships should be put in execution the night following ... So at about twelve of the clock that night six ships were brought and prepared ... having the wind and tide with them and their ordnance being charged were fired, and the men that were the executors, so soon as the fire was made they abandoned the ships and entered into five boats that were appointed for the saving of them. This matter did put such terror amongst the Spanish Army that they were fain [obliged] to let slip their cables and anchors and did work as it did appear great mischief amongst them ... then his Lordship with such as were with him did bear away after the Spanish fleet, the wind being at SSW and the Spanish fleet bare away in the NNE making into the depth of the channel and about ix of the clock in the morning we fell into position, then being within the water of Gravelines. They went into the proportion of a half moon, their admiral and viceadmiral were in the midst and their greatest vessels and power were one upon another ... The said wing found themselves as it did appear to be so charged that by making of haste to come into the body of their fleet some of them did entangle themselves one aboard the other ... [how] with honour they were beaten I will leave it to the report of some of the Spaniards that leapt into the seas and were taken up and are now in the custody of some of our fleet. The fight continued from ix of the clock until six of the clock at night, in the which time the Spanish Army bear away NNE and N by E as many as they could keeping company one with another. I assure your honour in very good order. Great was the spoil and harm that was done to them no doubt. I declare it unto your Lordship upon the credit of a poor gentleman that out of my ship there was shot 500 shot of demi-cannon, culverin [type of early cannon] and demi-culverin [smaller culverin with longer barrel and smaller bore], and when I was furthest off in discharging any quantity of the pieces, I was not out of the shot of their hagbuts [early muskets] and most times within speech one of another, and surely every man did well and as I have said no doubt the slaughter and hurt they received was great, as time will discover it.....

Mae it please yo[ur] honnor vppon Satturdaie the xxvij th of Julye, oure
Admerall the Lo[rd] Henry Seymour beinge w[i]th his fleet in the
morninge as Highe vp as betwene Donginot and Holstone attendinge
the cominge of the Armyes we there spake w[i]th dyvers shipps that
came from the west whoe saide they Sawe none of the Armyes
w[hi]ch put vs in hope oure Aduerall (beinge w[i]th in ij daies of
experience) that we myght beare into y[e] downes, to see if the
victualls were come to take in y[e] Same, So to be in a reddines
to do theire, but we had not byne Startedd there half an
hower, the wynde beinge at S.S.W.) but we recever a lett[er]
from the Lo[rd] Admerall by a pynnace declaringe vnto vs
what we should do, and forthow[i]th we made saile, gatte
out not havinge any tyme to releve owe selves w[i]th
victualls and bare over yo[u]r 4 to fromy toaste w[hi]ch we would
at the A[loofe] to drawe and by that tyme we could
recover over w[i]th was aboute vij of the clocke in the after
noune the Spanishe Armye was ancored to the Eastward
of Scales & lyes very rounde e newe togither not farre
from the Scares, oure Armye not beinge paste a myle e
half behinde them, whome I had recevered w[i]th my Shipp
did also caste ancer thwarte of a Co[m]pany of Scales & lodes e
immediatelie he Scent as my Lo[rd] Admerall, Shipp were come
to an ancer, his Lo[rd] Scent his pynnace aborde my Shipp
for me, w[i]th a messenger in y[e] Same, Comaundinge me
come aborde his Lo[rd] w[hi]ch I did e beinge aborde percevd
best the great e daungers of the Spanishe Armye, an
did consider that it was not possible to remove theme but
by advise of firinge of shipe w[hi]ch would make theme
to loose the only tyde w[hi]ch was apte e most fitt for owe
theire purpose, as also an occasion to put many of theme in
daunger of firinge e at the leaste to make theme to
lease theire Cables e anker w[hi]ch could not be lesse
then, ij for one; This I thoughte yt meet to acquainte
my Lo[rd] w[i]th all at my cominge to him, at that tyme w[hi]ch
was aboute vi of the clocke at nyghte and his Lo[rd] did like
very well of it e Saide the next daie he ho would
call a Councell, e put the Same in practise, e I do
were reasoninge of this matter in his Lo[rd] Cabbyn tarr[i]ed
theire w[i]th tyde aborde my Lo[rd] Shipp e[t]c ma his Shipp
the Beare e ij of ord we were all fange led togither
so as theire was Some inconvenience by breakinge of yardes

11
SP 12/214
(7)

MARIE
REINE
ESCOS·
SE

Two Queens in One Isle

MARY, QUEEN OF SCOTS

If there was one issue which caused Elizabeth more anguish and heart-searching than the decision to sign the Treaty of Nonsuch, and provoked more deceit, mind-changing and procrastination, it was the fate of Mary, Queen of Scots. The two women were in some ways rather similar: both were highly intelligent, and sexually frustrated (albeit in different ways); both were rulers in their own right. But there the similarities ended. Mary was the younger by nine years, and had suffered nothing like Elizabeth's formative experiences. She had also nothing like the Englishwoman's highly trained intellect, and when it came to the point she did not have her self discipline either.

Mary had grown up in the comfortable security of the French court, where, as first the espoused and then the wife of the Dauphin, she had been indulged in every way. In 1559, when she was seventeen, her father-in-law Henri II was killed in an accident, and her husband became François II. For about eighteen months she was Queen of France, but François was always a debilitated youth and her marriage was probably never consummated; then in December 1560 his ailments carried him off, and at the age of eighteen she was a widow and a dowager. The time had now come to return to her remote northern kingdom, of which she had in theory been queen since she was a few weeks old.

However, by the time that she landed at Leith in August 1561, Scotland was no longer the (more or less) Catholic country she had left in 1548. Thanks partly to Elizabeth, it was run by a council of Protestant nobles and had an established Calvinist Church. However, the position of the newly returned Queen was in some ways a strong one. No one disputed her title, and she had an excellent hereditary claim to the Crown of England as well. There was no

A miniature of Mary, Queen of Scots, by a follower of François Clouet.

chance of unseating Elizabeth, but unless or until the latter married and had children, she had every right to consider herself the heir. On this basis she could cause trouble for her cousin if she chose, and this was a useful bargaining counter. She declined to ratify the Treaty of Edinburgh with England, and waited on events.

In many respects Mary acted wisely, coming to terms with her Protestant subjects, without surrendering her own principles. But she was weakened by two circumstances. Her French kinsfolk, the Guises, were quickly embroiled in civil strife within France, and were in no position to come to her aid if she got into difficulties, and she was in urgent need of a husband. After Elizabeth she was the most eligible bride in Europe, and there was no shortage of suitors. The English Queen feared what choice she might make, and tried to interest her in the Earl of Leicester. Mary was insulted, and it looked as though she was about to play a strong hand. However, she then made a catastrophic mistake.

When the Earl of Lennox returned to Scotland after many years of English exile, he took with him his son, Henry, Lord Darnley. Darnley's mother, Margaret, was the daughter of Henry VIII's sister (Margaret Tudor) by her second marriage, so Darnley had a claim of his own to the English throne. However, it was not for that reason that Mary became interested in him; no sooner had she set eyes on this handsome young man, who was even taller than herself, than she fell hopelessly in love. Without consulting anything other than her own desires, she married him in 1565. Opinion in Scotland was divided; some pointed to his royal blood and approved, most did not, for a variety of reasons. A child was quickly conceived, but the relationship began and ended in bed. Darnley was vain, feckless and stupid, a serious liability as a King-Consort. He soon became involved in the factional politics for which

A sketch of the banner used by the Confederate Lords at the Battle of Carberry Hill, near Edinburgh, on 15 June 1567. It portrays Darnley's dead body, with the infant Prince James (later King James VI of Scotland and I of England) kneeling in prayer. The words 'Judge and avenge my cause, O Lord' appear above him.

Scotland was notorious, and was a participant in the murder of David Rizzio, Mary's Italian secretary. The birth of Prince James in June 1566 effected a temporary reconciliation, but by the end of the year the royal couple were more estranged than ever. Early in 1567, Darnley was murdered and the Queen was widely accused of complicity. These suspicions were confirmed when she hastily exonerated James Hepburn, Earl of Bothwell – generally believed to have been the actual assassin – created him Duke of Orkney and then married him after a staged abduction. Elizabeth's reaction to Mary's behaviour is clear in the letter she sent to her that summer; see document 13, *The errors of Mary Stuart*.

This extraordinary sequence of events, in which Mary's political judgement had been twice unseated by her desire for a man, led to her defeat, imprisonment in Loch Leven Castle, and forced abdication in favour of her infant son.

The errors of Mary Stuart

A letter from Elizabeth to Mary, Queen of Scots, 23 June 1567, sent by Robert Melville. This is a three-page clerk's draft, heavily corrected in Cecil's hand, but the tone of controlled contempt, almost disgust, is undoubtedly the Queen's.

The occasion was the receipt in England of the news of Mary's marriage on 15 May to James Hepburn, Earl of Bothwell. Mary's second husband Henry, Lord Darnley, whom she had created Duke of Albany, had been murdered in February 1567, and Bothwell was generally held responsible. There were rumours from the beginning that Mary was his accomplice. She had set up an enquiry which had exonerated him, but in which no one had any confidence. On 7 May, Bothwell divorced his wife, Jane Gordon, and on 12 May the Queen created him Duke of Orkney. She married him three days later after a staged abduction. There was widespread outrage in Scotland at this behaviour, and on 15 June, a week before this letter was written, Mary was defeated and captured at Carberry Hill by her indignant lords, and imprisoned in Loch Leven Castle. It appears that Elizabeth was aware of this when she wrote, but Mary's predicament aroused little sympathy. Bothwell escaped abroad.

ELIZABETH WROTE:

Madame,

It has been always held for a special principle in friendship that prosperity provides but adversity proves friends, whereof at this time finding occasion to verify the same with our actions, we have thought meet, both for our profession and your comfort, in these few word to testify our friendship, not only by admonishing you of the worst but to comfort you for the best. We have understood by your trusty servant Robert Melville such things as you gave him in charge to declare on your behalf concerning your estate, and specially of as much as could be said for the allowance of your marriage [to the Duke of Orkney]. Madame, to be plain with you, our grief has not been small that in this your marriage so slender consideration has been had that, as we perceive manifestly, no good friend you have in the whole world can like thereof, and if we should otherwise write or say we should abuse you. For how could a worse choice be made for your honour than in such haste to marry such a subject, who besides other and notorious lacks, public fame has charged with the murder of your late husband, besides the touching of yourself also in some part, though we trust that in that behalf falsely. And with what peril have you married him that has another lawful wife alive [Lady Jane Gordon, divorced 7 May 1567] whereby neither by God's law nor man's yourself can be his lawful wife, nor any children between you legitimate. This you see

The letter continues:

plainly, what we think of the marriage, whereof we are heartily sorry that we can conceive no better, what colourable reasons soever we have heard of your servant to induce us. We wish, upon the death of your husband, your first care had been to have searched and punished the murderers of our near cousin, your husband, which having been done effectually, as easily it might have been in a matter so notorious, there might have been many more things tolerated better in your marriage than now can be suffered to be spoken of. And surely we cannot but for friendship to yourself, besides the natural extinction that we have of blood to your late husband, profess ourselves earnestly bent to do anything in our power to procure the due punishment of that murder against any subject that you have, how dear so ever you should hold him. And next thereto, to be careful how your son the prince [James] may be preserved, for the comfort of yours and your realm, which two things we have from the beginning always taken to heart, and therein do mean to continue. And would be very sorry but you should allow us therein, what dangerous persuasions soever be made to you for the contrary.

Now for your estate in such adversity as we hear you should be – whereof we could not tell what to think to be true, having a great part of your nobility (as we hear) separated from you – we assure you that whatsoever we can imagine meet [suitable] for your honour and safety that shall lie in our power, we will perform the same that it shall well appear you have a good neighbour, a good sister, and a faithful friend, and so shall you undoubtedly always find and prove us to be indeed towards you. For which purpose we are determined to send with all speed one of our own trusty servants, not only to understand your state but also thereupon so to deal with your nobility and people as they shall find you not to lack our friendship and power for the preservation of your honour in quietness. And upon knowledge had what shall be further requisite to be done for your comfort and for the tranquility of your realm, we will omit no time to further the same, as you shall well see. And so we recommend ourselves to you, good sister, in as affectuous a manner as heretofore we were accustomed. At our manor of Richmond, the 23rd of June 1567.

Madame, it hath bene allweise held for a prynciple in frendshipp,
that prosperite provideth but adversite proueth frendes, wherof latt this
tyme fyndyng occasion to verefy the same wt our actions, we
have thought mete bothe for your comfort to our sincerite
profession and your comfort in these few words to
have our frendshipp to you not oly to comfort you by
yf it wast but to comfort you for yf by the was

we have understandly your servant Robert Melvill we have such
thynges as you gave hym in chardg to declare o your
behalf coecerniy your estate and specially to y allowaunce of
your mariadg. madame to be playne wt you our
grieff hath not bene small that ni your mariadg
but no more but y to make it allowable you at desire
to such reasons gather to git that it is as we
perceave manifestly no good frend you have in y whole world can lyke
therof, and if we shuld otherwise wryght or saye we shuld abuse
you for how could a worst choise be made for your honor
in such hast such a subiect who beside sundry notorious lackt
that to mary such gathek forde hath chargid wt
in mury of your late husbands deth beside y touching of your self also though we trust
firi y behalf falsly. and wt what shall have you
maryed hym y hath som other lawfull wif alyve, wherby neith
by Gods law nor mans your self ca be
his lefull wife, nor any childe betwixt you legitimat. This you se

Her courage and energy, however, were greatly superior to her wisdom. She escaped from Loch Leven, was defeated again, and fled across the border into England in 1568. Elizabeth was flabbergasted. Her first reaction was to seek her cousin's restoration, but it soon became apparent that to send Mary back to Scotland would be to send her to trial for murder, and probable execution.

Loch Leven Castle, Tayside.

DANGER TO ELIZABETH

As Elizabeth understood more of what had occurred, several thoughts predominated. The first was incredulity that Mary could have acted with such folly, but this incredulity was not untinged with sympathy. It had only been a few years earlier that Elizabeth had almost made a similar fool of herself over a man. The second was victory; here was a dangerous rival, delivered helplessly into her hands. The third was the consideration that Mary was a lawful sovereign, deposed and exiled by rebellious subjects; did she not have an obligation to help her? The Queen consulted long and earnestly with her Council. To send Mary back to Scotland would have been to send her to certain death, unless she was backed by a large English army, but such an intervention would

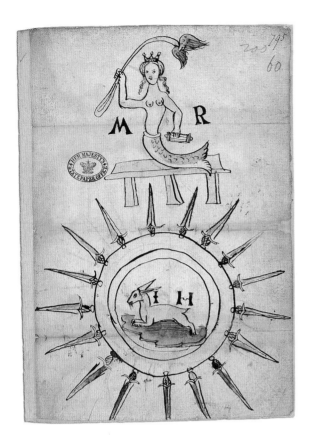

This allegorical sketch of Mary, Queen of Scots as a mermaid – a symbol of prostitution – would have been posted up in Edinburgh, c. June 1567.

have meant sacrificing all the gains which had been made in Anglo-Scottish relations since 1560. To send her to her kindred in France would have been to hand a powerful card to potential enemies. There really was no alternative to detaining her in England, difficult and dangerous as that might prove.

So began the nineteen-year saga of Mary's imprisonment. The danger to Elizabeth began almost at once, when the rebels of 1569 spoke of releasing Mary and espousing her cause, not in Scotland but in England. They came nowhere near achieving their objective (see document 14, *The rising in the north*) but they set up trains of thought and ambition. Opponents of William Cecil spoke of marrying Mary to the Duke of Norfolk, and persuading Elizabeth to recognize her as heir. The idea was not in itself treasonable, but the Queen was furious and Norfolk went to the block. As Mary gradually repaired her relations with the Catholic Church, she became the symbol of recusant dissent and ambition. Plots focused upon her – plots intended to destroy Elizabeth and put Mary upon the throne. Some she may not even have known about; others she certainly knew of and encouraged. From Ridolfi in 1571 to Babington in 1586, the English Council, and particularly Sir Francis Walsingham, built up a damning case against her, and pressure mounted both in Council and in Parliament for decisive action.

A letter from Queen Elizabeth to Henry Carey, Lord Hunsdon, Lord Warden of the East March against Scotland, congratulating him on his victory over the rebel Leonard Dacre, 26 February 1570. The postscript is written in Elizabeth's own hand.

This skirmish was the last incident in the rebellion of the northern earls, the main action of which had taken place in October and November 1569. Thomas Percy, Earl of Northumberland and Charles Neville, Earl of Westmorland, were disaffected to the extent of being opposed to the 1559 religious settlement, and deeply resentful of the power of William Cecil, whom they dismissed as a man of low birth. In the spring of 1569 they had supported plans to marry Mary, Queen of Scots to the Duke of Norfolk, and were exposed to Elizabeth's anger when she made her reaction to that proposal plain. At the same time, there was a radical Catholic conspiracy among some of their followers to depose Elizabeth in Mary's favour, with Spanish help. It is not clear that either of the Earls supported this, but their behaviour had left them so exposed that they felt they had no option but to take up arms. There was little support outside County Durham and the North Riding, and no Spanish help arrived.

After advancing into Yorkshire, about the 25th of November the rebels began to retreat, and on the 30th they dispersed, the Earls escaping into Scotland.

Leonard Dacre had a different grievance, because he was the claimant to an inheritance which had passed to the Duke of Norfolk. In January 1570 he tried to revive the rebellion with Scottish help, but was caught and defeated by Hunsdon before his allies could join him. Hunsdon was the son of Mary Carey (née Boleyn), Anne's sister, and hence the Queen's full cousin.

ELIZABETH WROTE:

By the Queen.

Right trusty and well-beloved cousin, we greet you well. And right glad we are that it has pleased God to assist you in this your late service against that cankered subtle traitor Leonard Dacre, whose force, being far greater in number than yours, we perceive you have overthrown, and how he thereupon was the first that fled, having at it seems a heart readier to show his unloyal falsehood and malice than to abide the fight. And though the best we could have desired was to have had him taken, yet we thank God that he is in this sort overthrown, and forced to flee our realm to his like company of rebels, whom we doubt not but God of his favourable justice will confound with such ends as are meet for them. We will not now by words express how inwardly glad we are that you have had such success, whereby both your courage in such an unequal match, your faithfulness towards us, and your wisdom is seen to the world, this your act being the very first that ever was executed by fight in field in our time against any rebels. But we mean also in deeds by just reward to let the world see how much we esteem and can consider such a service as this is. And so we would have yourself also thank God heartily, as we doubt not but you do (from whom all victories do proceed) and comfort yourself with that assurance of our most favourable acceptation. We have also herewith sent our letter of thanks to Sir John Forster [the Deputy Warden]

and would have you namely thank our good faithful soldiers of Berwick, in whose worthy service we do repose no small trust. 26 February 1569 [1570].

In Elizabeth's own hand:

I doubt much, my Harry, whether that the victory were given me more joyed me or that you were by God appointed the instrument of my glory, and I assure you for my country's good the first might suffice, but for my heart's contentation the second more pleased me. It likes me not a little that with a good testimony of your faith, there is seen a stout courage of your mind that more trusted to the goodness of your quarrel than to the weakness of your numbers. Well I can say no more. *Beatus est ille servus quem cum Dominus venerit invenerit faciendo sua mandata.* [Blessed is that servant who, when the Lord comes, He will discover doing His commands.] And that you may not think that you have done nothing for your profit, though you have done much for your honour, I intend to make this journey somewhat to increase your livelihood, that you may not say to yourself, *Perditur quod factum est ingrato.* [It is lost because it was done for an ingrate.]

Your loving kinswoman,

Elizabeth R.

By the Quene

Right trustie and welbiloud cousin we grete you well And
right glad we ar, that it hath pleased God to assist you in this
your late servire against that ranked subtil traitor Leonard
Dacre, whose forre, being farr greater in nombre then yours
we perceave you have overthrowen, and how he Grippon was
he first that fled having as it semeth a hart readyer to showe
his unloyall falsehed and malice, then to abyde the fight And
though, the best we could have desyred, was to have him takē:
yet we thank God, that he is in this sort overthrowen, and
forred to flee our realm to his like company of rebells. whom we
doubt not but God of his favorable Justice will conforme with
suche endes as ar mete for them, We will not now by
woordes expres how inwardly glad we ar that you have had
suche successe wherby bothe your courage in such an inequall matter
your faithfulnes toward us and your wisdom is seen to the
worold, this your act being the very furst that ever was don with
by fight in feld in our tyme against any rebells; but we meane
also in dede by Just reward to lett the world see, how muche
we esteme and can consider suche a servire as this is, And so we
would have yourself also thank God hartly, as we doubt not but
you do (from whom all victorie do procede) and confort yourself
with the assurance of our moost favorable acceptation. We have
also herewith sent our lre of thanks to Sr John Forster, and would
have you namely, thank our good faithfull souldiours of Barwik
in whose worthy prowes we do repose no small trust. 26 febr 156

I dowte much, My harry whither that the victory were geven me
more ioyed me or that yow were by God apoynted the instrument of
my glory, and I assure yow for my cotreys good the first might suffice
but for my harts contentation the second more pleasd me It likes me
not a litle that wt a good testimony of yor faith there is seen a stowte
courage of yor mind that more trusted to the godnes of yor quarrell
than to the weakenes of yor nombor well I can say no more, beatus
est ille servus quem Domino veniens invenerit faciendo sua mandata
And that yow may not think that yow have don nothing for your
proffitt though yow have don much for yor honr I entend to make
this journey somewhat to encrease your livelood that you may not say
to yorself perditur quod factū est ingrato.

263   Your loving kinneswoman Elizab

Elizabeth was profoundly disturbed. She recognized the danger, and also felt deeply contemptuous of a woman who was not only foolish enough to throw away her whole position, but indiscreet enough to expose her intrigues to the scrutiny of her enemies. On the other hand, she was an anointed queen, and Elizabeth was by no means certain that she had any right, legal or moral, to take action against her. She was also in a position not unlike that which Elizabeth herself had experienced in her sister's reign. She was the 'second person', whose name was on every malcontent's lips, whether she wished it or not. However, there was a big difference. If Elizabeth had ever intrigued actively against her sister, her activities left no trace, whereas Mary's letters were copied for all to read. Eventually the logic of events broke down the Queen's

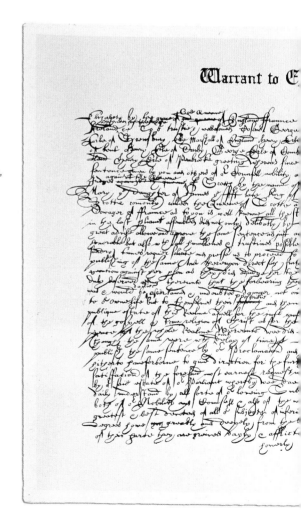

The execution warrant for Mary, Queen of Scots, reluctantly signed by Elizabeth in February 1587.

resistance. She accepted the Bond of Association (which licensed lynch law against anyone who plotted against the Queen), and thus ensured that neither Mary nor anyone else could seize her Crown by covert assassination. She then allowed a special commission to pronounce upon Mary's guilt in the Babington Plot, and proclaimed their verdict (see document 15, *One conspiracy too many*). Finally, in 1587 she sent her *bête noire* to the block, but with such an uneasy conscience that she immediately attempted to shift the responsibility onto almost anyone who happened to be standing by. However, the sky did not fall, and Elizabeth enjoyed the benefit of a new surge of loyalty and popularity. For that, most prices were worth paying.

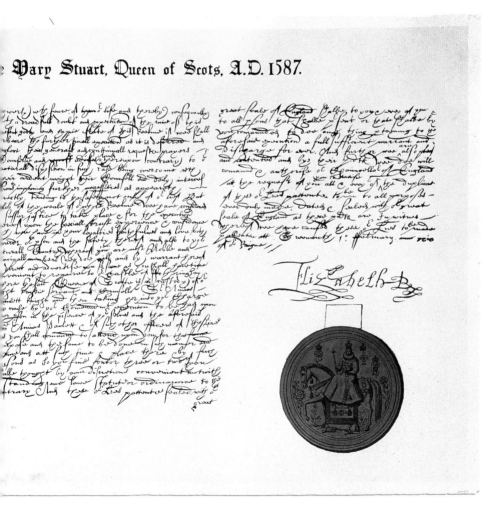

Mary Stuart, Queen of Scots, A.D. 1587.

15 *One conspiracy too many*

This is the opening passage from a copy of the proclamation declaring the sentence against Mary, Queen of Scots, printed by Christopher Barker who was 'printer to the Queen's most excellent Majesty'. It is dated 4 December 1586, and was publicly read out by city officials at Cheapside Cross, and other locations around London, on 6 December.

Mary's ultimate downfall had come about through her implication in the Babington plot earlier that year. The conspiracy, organized by Mary's former page, had planned to murder Elizabeth, rescue Mary from captivity and rally support among English Catholics for a Spanish invasion force. Walsingham had intercepted letters proving Mary's involvement, and a special commission had been convened at Fotheringhay to hear her defence. Mary had denied both the competence of the commission and her own complicity in the plot, but she had been found guilty.

This proclamation by Elizabeth formally announces and justifies the judgement against Mary. The Queen claims to be 'deeply grieved' that she has been betrayed by her own 'sex and blood', and that she was reluctant to bring Mary to trial. The proceedings of the special commission are then explained and the proclamation announces Mary's guilt: '...the said Mary, pretending title to the same Crown, had compassed and imagined within the same realm divers things tending to the hurt, death and destruction of our royal person...'. The sentence of death was implicit.

THE PROCLAMATION:

By the Queen,

A true copy of the proclamation lately published by the Queen's Majesty under the Great Seal of England, for the declaring of the sentence, lately given against the Queen of Scots, in form as following.

Elizabeth, by the grace of God, Queen of England, France and Ireland, Defender of the faith, etc. Whereas we were given to understand very credibly (though to our great grief) that divers things were and of late time have been compassed, imagined, and resolutely intended tending directly to the hurt and destruction of our royal person and to the subversion of the estate of our realm by foreign invasions and rebellions at home, as well by the Queen of Scots remaining in our realm under our protection as by many divers other wicked persons [the Babington plotters] with her privity, who had freely confessed the same and had thereupon received open trial, judgement and execution according to the laws for their desserts; and though in very truth we were greatly and deeply grieved in our mind to think or imagine that any such unnatural and monstrous acts should be either devised or willingly assented unto against us by her, being a princess born, and of our sex and blood, and one also whose life and honour we had many times before saved and preserved: yet were we so directly drawn to think all the same to be true by the sight and understanding of such proofs as were manifestly produced before us upon matters that had as well proceeded from herself as from the conspirators themselves, who voluntarily and freely without any coercion had confessed their conspirations both jointly with her and directed by her, against our person and our realm; and therefore also we saw great reason to think the same over dangerous to be suffered to pass onward to take their full effect.

Wherefore we were, by sundry lords of our nobility and others our loving subjects, earnestly moved and counselled to take undelayed order for the inquisition and examination of all these dangerous enterprises and conspiracies by sundry ways directly avowed to be by the said Queen of Scots against us and our realm certainly intended, and also to use all present means with expedition to withstand or rather prevent the same. And for that we were very unwilling to proceed against her, considering her birth and estate, by such usual sort as by the common laws of the realm we might have lawfully done (which was by indictment and arraignment by ordinary juries): therefore, in respect both of our own honour and of her person, we yielded, by good advice given to us, to proceed in the most honourable sort that coulds be devised within our realm to the examination hereof, according to a late act of parliament made the 23rd day of November in the 27th year of our reign [27 Elizabeth c.1] ...

❧ By the Queene.

❧ A true Copie of the Proclamation

lately published by the Queenes Maiestie, vnder the great
Seale of England, for the declaring of the Sentence,
lately giuen against the Queene of Scottes,
in fourme as followeth.

Lizabeth, by the grace of God, Queene of England, France and Ireland, defender of the faith, &c. Whereas we were giuen to vnderstand verie credibly, (though to our great griefe,) that diuers things were, and of late time had beene compassed, imagined and resolutely intended, tending directly to the hurt and destruction of our Royal person, and to the subuersion of the Estate of our Realme, by forrein inuasions, & rebellions at home, aswell by the Queene of Scottes, remaining in our Realme vnder our Protection, as by many diuers other wicked persons with her priuitie, who had freely confessed the same, and had thereupon receiued open triall, Iudgement and Execution according to the lawes for their desertes: And though, in verie trueth we were greatly and deepely grieued in our minde, to thinke or imagine that any such vnnatural & monstrous Acts should be either deuised, or willingly assented vnto against vs, by her being a Princesse borne, and of our sexe and blood, and one also whose life & honor we had many times before saued and preserued: Yet were we so directly drawne to thinke all the same to be true, by the sight and vnderstanding of such prooses, as were manifestly produced afore vs, vpon matters that had as wel proceeded from her selfe, as from the conspiratos themselues, who voluntarilie and freelie without any coertion had confessed their conspirations, both ioyntly with her, and directed by her, against our Person and our Realme, and thersore also we saw great reason, to thinke the same ouer daungerous, to be suffered to passe onwarde to take their full effecte. Wherefore, we were by sundrie Lordes of our Nobilitie, and others our louing subiectes, earnestly mooued and counselled, to take vndelaied order, for the inquisition and examination of all these dangerous enterprises, and conspiracies by sundrie waies directly auowed to be by the sayde Queene of Scottes, against vs and our Realme certainely intended, and also to vse all present meanes with expedition, to withstand, or rather to preuent the same, And for that we were verie vnwilling to proceede against her, considering her birth and Estate, by such vsuall sort as by the common lawes of the Realme, we might haue lawfullie done, which was, by inditement and arraignment by ordinarie Iuries: therefore, in respect both of our owne honour, and of her person, we yeelded, by good aduise giuen to vs, to proceede in the most honourable sort that coulde be deuised within our Realme to the examination hereof, according to a late Acte of Parliament made the xxiii. day of Nouember, in the xxviii. yeere of our Reigne. Whereupon by our Commission vnder our great Seale of Englande, bearing Date at our Castle of Windsor in our Countie of Barkshire, the sixt day of October nowe last past, we did for that purpose, according to the saide Statute, assigne, name, and appoynt all the Lordes and others of our Priuie counsaile, and so many other Earles and Barons Lordes of Parliament, of the greatest degree and most ancient of the Nobilitie of this our Realme, as with the same Lordes and others of our priuie counsell, made vp the nomber of fourtie and two, adding also thereto a further nomber, according to the tenour of the foresaide Acte of Parliament, of certaine of the chiefest and other principall Iudges of the Courtes of Recorde at Westminster, amounting in the whole to the number of fourtie and seuen, to examine all things compassed and imagined, tending to the hurt of our Royall person, as well by the saide Queene of Scottes, by the name of Marie, the daughter and heire of Iames the fifth, late King of Scottes, commonly called the Queene of Scottes & Dowager of France, as by any other by her priuitie, & all the circumstances thereof, and thereupon, according to the tenor of ye said Act of Parliament, to giue sentence or iudgement, as vpon

NON SINE SOLE
IRIS.

Gloriana, the Virgin Queen

IMAGE AND POWER

As the Count of Feria had pointed out at the very outset of her reign, Elizabeth loved the plaudits of the multitude. This was partly simple vanity; she loved the mendacious flattery of her courtiers and their poet friends. But it was also shrewd politics. Elizabeth was not a war-lord, who could command the allegiance of men by the example of leadership and physical courage. She could bewilder and even intimidate her individual servants by calculated displays of femininity, but that would not give her broad-based support. Elizabeth was very conscious of the fact that her regime rested ultimately on consent. During her reign, this was not focused exclusively in Parliament, as it later became. Certain types of action – the levying of direct taxes, for example – did require the consent of Parliament, but much did not. This was called prerogative: its limits were not clearly defined, and the Queen took good care that they should not be. However, at the end of the day her coercive resources, even intangible ones, were limited. Laws had to be both enforced and obeyed, and policies endorsed, willingly by most of the people most of the time, otherwise the country became ungovernable. There had been hints of that in both 1536, with Henry's break with Rome and 1549, with Edward's First Act of Uniformity, and *Book of Common Prayer*. Elizabeth had sailed close to the wind in the first decade of her reign with her Protestant Church settlement, but that had been a matter of conscience, and she had got away with it. Moreover, after the Pope declared her a heretic in 1570, it was no longer really an issue.

This detailed plan of the market square in Barking, Essex, c. 1595, reflects its importance as the economic and judicial centre, not only of the town but also of the surrounding area. The 'town-house' is central, incorporating the corn-market with its bushel, and various buildings of the local legal system: the court-house, justices' chamber, and stock-house (a prison where offenders were set in stocks).

Shops line the remaining three sides of the square, with the well and weights and scales shown on the right. The pillory, a very public instrument of punishment, is prominent in the foreground.

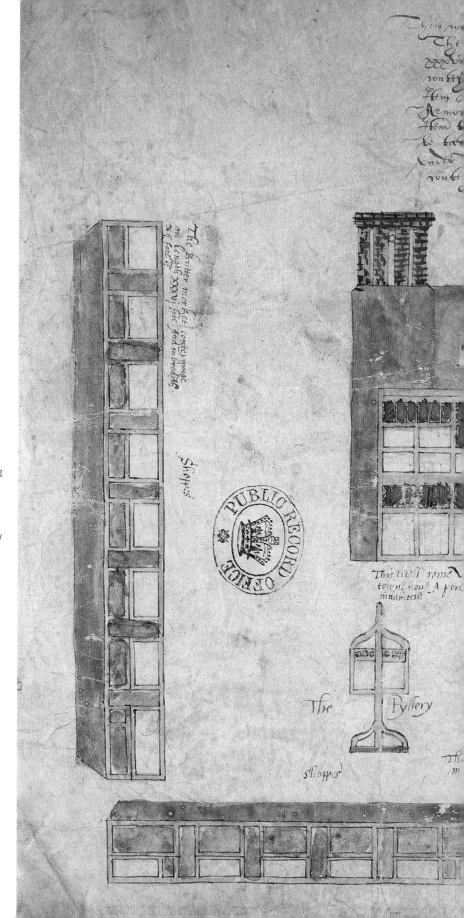

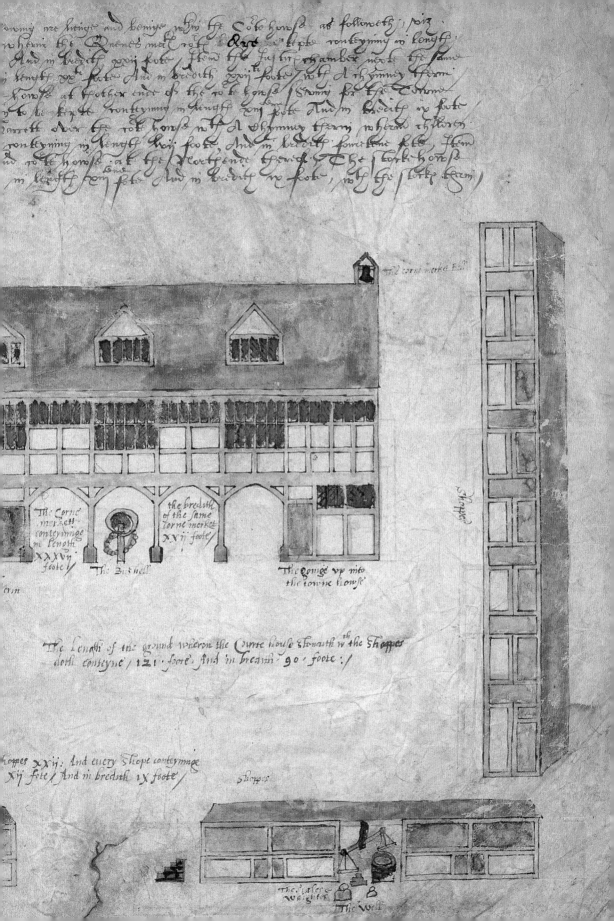

The corne market Bell

The Corne merkett conteyninge in length XXXVIJ foote

The Bushell

the bredth of the same corne merket XVIJ foote

The gowge vp into the towne howse

The Length of the ground wheron the Curte house & lowaith wth the Shoppes doth conteyne 121 foote And in breadth 90 foote

Shoppes XXIJ And every Shope conteyninge XIJ fote And in bredth IX foote

Shoppes

Shoppes

The Butchers Waightes

The Well

Popular government was also cheap government. With noblemen competing for the favour of a smile (metaphorically at least), and country gentlemen striving to climb the pecking order of the Commission of the Peace and to place their sons and daughters at court, there was no need to be lavish with land grants and annuities. With her loyal subjects lining her ways to cheer and shout 'God save your Grace', there were no rebellions to be expensively suppressed. However, the Queen was also aware that she needed freedom of action if her prerogative was not to become meaningless. Thanks largely to her father, she was free from the overwhelming pressure of noble consensus which had sometimes afflicted her medieval predecessors, but a gentry consensus could be almost equally constricting if it was not carefully managed. Nor were the people at large an entirely negative force. Yeoman officers, such as constables, headboroughs and church wardens, were the backbone of social stability. They also provided the best soldiers and under-officers, both for the army and the navy; and as merchants and craftsmen they generated much of the community's prosperity. So although in theory they had no voice in national politics, in practice they were men to be counted. Elizabeth knew all this perfectly well, and her carefully crafted image was an economical and effective way of generating the degree of consensus which she needed. Evidence of Elizabeth's skills as a politician is revealed in her 'golden speech' of 1601 (document 16, *A rhetorical device*).

At first there were two essential ingredients: Englishness and her father's memory. Henry may have been brutal and eccentric, but he was remembered as the man who had made England independent and great. He had thrown out the Italian priests, and fought the French to a standstill. There was a good deal of collective amnesia about this, but when someone cried out 'Remember good old King Henry VIII' as she rode to her coronation, he was

Illuminated initial membrane, with portrait of Elizabeth I, Court of King's Bench: *Coram Rege* Roll (Hilary Term, 1581).

Extracts from an eight-page summary of Elizabeth's 'golden speech', 30 November 1601, printed in London by Robert Barker. Whether this copy was authorized or not is unknown.

The occasion for this speech was the agitation which had been going on in the House of Commons on the subject of Patents of Monopoly. These were grants of control over some aspect of manufacturing or trade, usually given to courtiers or other royal servants by way of reward. The recipient did not normally either trade or manufacture himself, but rather sold licences to those who did. They then passed on the cost to their customers in enhanced prices. It was these price increases which fuelled the controversy. The reason for such an expedient was that the Queen was desperately short of money, and unwilling to ask for larger taxes. Instead of rewarding her servants directly, therefore, she developed this way of enabling them to reward themselves at the public expense. When the strength of feeling against monopolies became clear, Elizabeth professed innocence, and took refuge behind her good intentions.

This speech was a rhetorical masterpiece, very strong on emotional appeal, but doing almost nothing to address the specific grievances. Although Elizabeth's speeches were often drafted by her secretaries, the words eventually delivered – and the ideas – were her own; this particular speech is a fair example of her instinctive evasiveness.

THE TEXT READS:

Her majesty's most princely answer delivered by herself at the court at Whitehall, on the last day of November, 1601, when the speaker of the Lower House of Parliament, assisted with the greatest part of the knights and burgesses, had presented their humble thanks for her free and gracious favour in preventing and reforming of sundry grievances by abuse of many grants commonly called monopolies. The same being taken verbatim in writing by A.B. [probably Anthony Blagrave], as near as he could possibly set it down. Imprinted at London, anno 1601.

Mr. Speaker, we perceive by you, whom we did constitute the mouth of our Lower House, how with even consent they are fallen into the due consideration of the precious gift of thankfulness, most usually least esteemed where it is best deserved. And therefore we charge you tell them how acceptable such sacrifice is, worthily received of a loving king who doubts much whether the given thanks can be of more poise [weight] than the owed is to them. And suppose that they have done more for us than they themselves believe. And this is our reason: who keeps their sovereign from the lapse of error, in which, by ignorance and not by intent they might have fallen, what thank they deserve, we know, though you may guess. And as nothing is more dear to us than the loving conservation of our subjects' hearts, what an undeserved doubt might we have incurred if the abusers of our liberality, the thrallers ['those who enslave'] of our people, the wringers of the poor, had not been told us! Which, before our heart or hand should agree unto, we wish we had neither, and do thank you the more, supposing that such griefs touch not some amongst you in particular. We trust there resides in their conceits of us no such simple care of their good, whom we so dearly prize, that our hand should pass aught that might injure any, though they doubt not it is lawful for our kingly state to grant gifts of sundry sorts of whom we make election, either for service done or merit to be deserved, as being for a king to make choice on whom to bestow benefits, more to one than another.

You must not beguile yourselves, nor wrong us, to think that the glossy lustre of a glittering glory of a king's title may so extol us that we think all is

The text continues:

lawful what we list, nor caring what we do. Lord, how far should you be off from our conceits! For our part we vow unto you that we suppose physicians' aromatical savours, which in the top of their potion they deceive the patient with, or gilded drugs that they cover their bitter sweet with, are not more beguilers of senses than the vaunting boast of a kingly name may deceive the ignorant of such an office. I grant that such a prince as cares but for the dignity, nor passes not how the reins be guided, so he rule – to such a one it may seem an easy business. But you are cumbered [afflicted] (I dare assure) with no such prince, but such a one as looks how to give account before another tribunal seat than this world affords ...

DIEV ET MON DROIT

Imprinted at London.

151

HER MAIESTIES

most Princely answere, deliuered
by her selfe at the Court at *Whitehall*, on
the last day of Nouember 1601. When the
Speaker of the Lower House of Parliament (assisted
with the greatest part of the Knights, and Burgesses) had presented their humble thanks for her free and gracious fauour, in preuenting and reforming of sundry grie-
uances, by abuse of many grants, commonly
called MONOPOLIES: The same being taken *Verbatim* in writing by A.B.
as neere as he could possibly
set it downe.

M. Speaker,

E perceiue
by you, *whome*
we did constitute
the mouth of our
Lower House,
howe with euen
consent they are
fallen into the due consideration of the
A 3   *precious*

2

precious gift of thankefulnesse, most v-
sually least esteemed, where it is best
deserued. And therefore we charge
you tell them how acceptable such sacrifice is woorthily receiued of a louing
King, who doubteth much whether the
giuen thanks can be of more poise then
the owed is to them: and suppose that
they haue done more for vs, then they
themselues beleeue. And this is our
reason: Who keepes their Souereigne
from the lapse of error, in which, by ignorance, and not by intent, they might
haue fallen; what thanke they deserue,
we know, though you may gesse. And as
nothing is more deere to vs then the louing coseruation of our subiects hearts,
What an vndeserued doubt might we
haue incurred, if the abusers of our
liberality, the thrallers of our people,
       the

3

the wringers of the poore, had not bene
tolde vs! which, ere our heart or hand
should agree vnto, we wish we had neither: and do thanke you the more, supposing that such griefes touch not some
amongst you in particular. We trust
there resides, in their conceits of vs, no
such simple cares of their good, whome
we so deerly prise, that our hand should
passe ought that might iniure any,
though they doubt not it is lawfull for
our kingly state to grant gifts of sundry
sorts of whō we make election, either for
seruice done, or merit to be deserued, as
being for a King to make choise on whō
to bestow benefits, more to one then another. You must not beguile your selues,
nor wrong vs, to thinke that the glosing
lustre of a glistring glory of a Kings
title may so extoll vs, that we thinke all
       ii

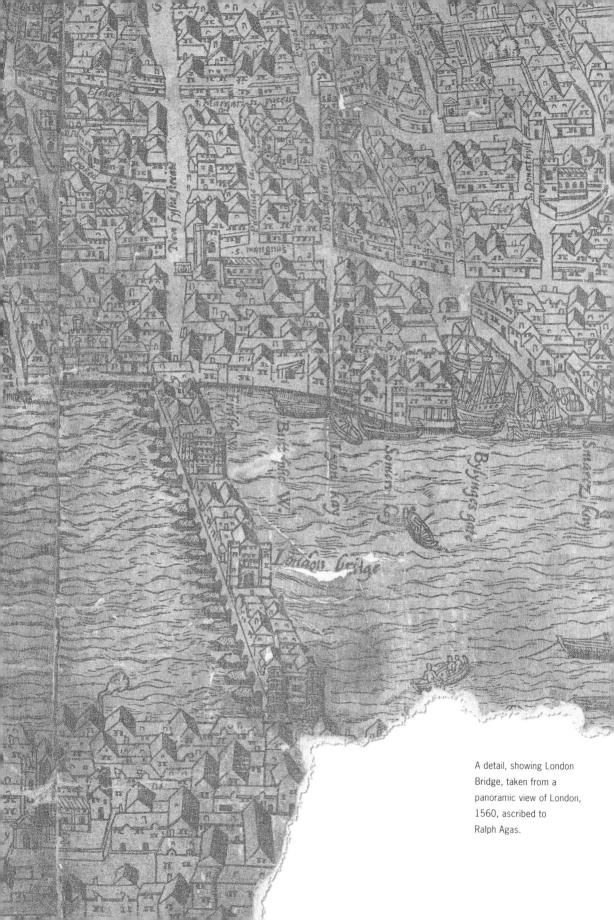

A detail, showing London Bridge, taken from a panoramic view of London, 1560, ascribed to Ralph Agas.

expressing (perhaps intentionally) a popular view. Feria observed very quickly that she was much more feared than her sister '...and has her way absolutely, as her father did'. He added that she 'gloried' in her father, and it was a significant observation – especially as Feria did not like her, or what she stood for.

Elizabeth described herself as 'mere English', and this was widely celebrated in popular ballads and tracts. Mary had been half Spanish, and most of the woes of her reign were (quite unfairly) ascribed to that fact. It had not been Mary's religion which had made her unpopular, except in a few places, like London, but the feeling that she was abandoning English for Habsburg priorities. It was that tendency which Elizabeth was expected to reverse, and she knew it. She also used the obvious metaphor of marriage; she was the bride of her country. 'Come over the bourne, Bessy' had sung her 'lover England' in the popular ballad of 1559, professing a hope and a lifelong allegiance which were to prove strangely prophetic. There was nothing original about this; her sister had used the same image, and had not abandoned it when she found a human husband. However, it had lacked impact as Mary had struggled to reconcile her priorities as wife and sovereign. Because Elizabeth remained unmarried, the image gained in significance for her, until at last the removal of her 'wedding ring' shortly before her death, for purely practical reasons, was taken to symbolize the impending dissolution of the union.

A pair of gloves presented to Elizabeth on her visit to Oxford University in 1566. Elizabeth was fond of fine clothes and jewellery.

Other images which are historically associated with Elizabeth arose later, as circumstances changed. Deborah was an early one, exclusive to Protestant hopefuls. Female images of

One of a number of versions, this poem (in the middle section of the page) is taken from a Commonplace Book (an early type of reference book) compiled by Henry Stanford, a servant of Henry Carey, Lord Hunsdon. It is ascribed to Elizabeth by contemporary report rather than conclusive evidence, though it is highly probable that she composed it.

Elizabeth is known to have written verses of this sort, often in ironic exchanges with members of her court, and the sentiment is certainly appropriate. It also displays the kind of personal vanity, which she more usually displayed in response to the flattery of her courtiers.

The poem probably dates from the early 1580s, when she had finally abandoned the marriage negotiation with the Duke of Anjou – her last attempt at matrimony. The other poem transcribed here, *On Monsieur's Departure*, was written in about 1582, and is in the same vein. As 'Monsieur' was Anjou's official designation in France, it is more than likely that the poem refers to him.

ELIZABETH'S VERSE:

When I was fair and young, and favour graced me,
Of many was I sought their mistress for to be.
But I did scorn them all, and answered them therefore:

'Go, go, go, seek some otherwhere;
    Importune me no more.'

But there fair Venus' son, that brave victorious boy,
Said, 'What, you scornful dame, since that you are so coy',
I will so wound your heart, that you shall learn therefore:

'Go, go, go seek some otherwhere;
    Importune me no more.'

But then I felt straightaway a change within my breast,
The day unquiet was; the night I could not rest.
For I did sore repent that I had said before:

'Go, go, go seek some otherwhere;
    Importune me no more.'

On Monsieur's Departure

I grieve and dare not show my discontent,
I love and yet am forced to seem to hate
I do, yet dare not say I ever meant
I seem stark mute but inwardly do prate [speak inadvisedly]
I am and not, I freeze and yet am burned
Since from myself another self I turned

My care is like my shadow in the sun
Follows me flying, flies when I pursue it
Stands and lies by me, does what I have done
His too familiar care does make me rue it
No means I find to rid him from my breast
Till by the end of things it be suppressed

Some gentler passion slide into my mind
For I am soft and made of melting snow
Or be more cruel, love, and so be kind
Let me or float or sink [whether I float or sink], be high or low
Or let me live with some more sweet content
Or die and so forget what love ever meant

Fayre phillis is the sheapheards queene, was neber queene so faire as shee
& Coridon her only swayne was neber sure a swayne as hee
Sweete phillis sate the fowlest fare that eber yet did eye behold
& Coridon the constantest faike yt eber yet kept lambes in fold
fair phillis hath the fondst wit yt eber yt she wode did breed
& Coridon the herwost hart yt eber yt were sheapheards weedi
Sweete phillis is the only sweete that eber yet yt wode did yeld
& Coridon the kyndest swayne yt eber yet did keepe the feild
Sphilomita is phillis bird though the Coridon be hee yt taught her
& Coridon did feare her sing though phillida be shee yt taught her
the little lambes are phillis loue yet Coridon is hee yt feede them
the gardens roses are phillis growinge yet Coridon is hee yt weede them
poore Coridon dote keepe the feild though phillida be shee yt sowes them
& phillida dote make the meades but Coridon is shee yt mowes them
Since then that phillis onely is the only sheapheard & only queene
& Coridon her only swayne that only hath a sheapheard byn
though phillis keepe the bowere of state, shall Coridon runne away
no sheapheard go woode out the weeke & sunday shalbe holiday

when I was fayre & yonge & fauour graced me
of many was I sought yt made mee thei[r] to be
but I did scorne them all & said to them therfore
go go goe seeke som otherwhere importune me no more
but there fair Uenus sonne, yt braha Uictorious boy
said what then stowersull dame site yt thou art so roy
I will so wound thei hart, yt then shalt learne therfore
go go go seeke som otherwhere importune me no more
but then I felt straightt way a chounge with in my brest
the day unquiet was the night, I could not rest
for I did sore repent, that I had said before
go go go seeke som otherwhere importune me no more.

I must what wole she did she meane: my proofe true kyndnes to forsake
that causeles feare will cause les loue, & yeeldes rawe to ill rawe les mak[e]
for to be trusted makes on true & falshood is suspicion due.

In thinking that thou wouldest not fynd, thou maist fynd that thou wouldst not sholde
and by mistrust makes her but trud, when trust hath tried true & meada
for feare of faith makes fait to feare, a sharpe edged tole no ill will beare

Loue me then maist but for the best, & rate me oft but on the sharr
hope me then maist but for my rest, & bowe my ioyes to breede me more
doe onely in this thie good meede, that then wilt proue for eber good.

power were rare, particularly in the bible which described a very male-dominated society, but there were a few: Judith for the warrior woman who struck blows for the faith, and Deborah for the woman who sat in judgement by the Lord's command. It is unlikely that the Queen invented, or discovered, this one for herself, but it was appropriate, and features as early as the coronation pageantry. There was, however, no suggestion that Deborah was beautiful, or sexually charged – quite the reverse – and Elizabeth's popular image at first made little use of sexual symbolism, except in the metaphor of marriage. It was her courtiers who praised her beauty, and did so all the more enthusiastically when her real appearance had been marred by a smallpox attack in 1562, which had left her scarred and half bald. From the age of twenty-nine the real Elizabeth relied upon wigs and cosmetics for her beauty, although she had good features and this was not entirely an artifice until much later. Document 17, *Regrets*, perhaps reflects Elizabeth's view of herself.

The big change, or watershed, in the Queen's image came in the late 1570s and early 1580s coinciding, more or less, with the end of hopes, or fears, for her marriage. Sir Henry Lee developed the Accession Day tilts, which cast her in the role of the Fairy Queen, from 1578 when it was becoming necessary to find appropriate secular festivities to replace the banned celebrations of the Old Church. By 1588, exploiting her own taste for pastoral fantasies, she was being presented as Belphoebe or Astraea, and after the Armada victory, increasingly as Gloriana. It was at this time also that she became the Virgin Queen, for reasons which we have already noted. Virginity was not only a symbol of integrity, it was also a symbol of power. Elizabeth did not lead armies into battle, despite dressing up in armour in 1588; one of the reasons why she so disliked war was that it gave power to the men who did. One of the most revealing, and discreditable, episodes of her reign was the manner in which she dealt with her old friend the Earl of Leicester when she sent him to the Low Countries, and recalled him in disfavour for using the discretion which she had allowed him (see document 18, *Leicester rebuked*, to see exactly how Elizabeth treated him). However, a woman did not have to be a warrior to be an inspiration, and

The Queen's last favourite,
Robert Devereux, second
Earl of Essex (c. 1596),
by Marcus Gheeraerts
the Younger.

that was the objective of much late Elizabethan imagery; the main purpose of the Virgin Queen. As her country became weary, and a shade cynical about her posturings, the image promotion became more strenuous. How long this could have continued we do not know, because the old Queen died before her waxwork had time to melt.

ELIZABETH AND ESSEX

In the last decade of her life, Elizabeth may even have become self-deceived, so long had she been acting a part. Whereas her treatment of Leicester in 1586, although it distressed him greatly, did not destroy their relationship, her dealing with the Earl of Essex in 1599 was disastrous for both of them. Essex, born in 1566, was actually Leicester's stepson, and was introduced to the court by him while he was still an adolescent. He was handsome, dashing, and not without ability both political and military. Unfortunately he was also entirely without self awareness or self discipline, incurably ambitious and displayed a strong paranoid streak. After Leicester's death in 1588, he became a sort of substitute. In a sense he was the ageing Queen's toy-boy, but there was never any suggestion of a sexual relationship. He was a brilliant and amusing conversationalist, a skilled card player, and generally good company. On this basis he was able to behave with a lack of restraint, and even common courtesy, that councillors and other courtiers alike found deeply offensive. The Queen, however, regularly forgave him these outbursts on the grounds of his youth, and the extravagant penitence which he always professed.

18 *Leicester rebuked*

A letter from Elizabeth to the Earl of Leicester, in response to news that he had accepted the Governor General-ship of the Low Countries, 10 February 1586. This is taken from a clerk's copy.

The situation in the Low Countries had been troubling Elizabeth for many years. Full scale rebellion against the Spanish regency government had broken out in 1572, after several years of sporadic resistance and repression. At first there were two issues: provincial and noble privileges, and religion. In 1579, however, the ten Catholic provinces of the south had made their peace with Spain, leaving the seven Protestant provinces of the north to continue what was rapidly becoming a war of independence. Elizabeth disliked rebels, and disliked the kind of Calvinists which the Dutch were becoming, but it was vital to England's security that Spain should not gain control of the Dutch ports. In 1584 the Dutch leader, William of Orange, was assassi-nated, and it seemed that the revolt must be suppressed unless it secured outside help. Elizabeth tried very hard to secure her own aims without open intervention or commitment, but this proved impossible and in August 1585 she signed the Treaty of Nonsuch. By that treaty she was com-mitted to sending immediate military and financial help, and a commander of status and experience to represent her.

She chose the Earl of Leicester, and he believed that he had been given discretion to act on her behalf. Believing full English commitment to be essential, he accepted the proferred position of Governor General. Elizabeth was furious, having no intention of accepting the implied responsibility, or getting involved in the internal politics of the provinces. This letter, delivered by the Queen's special envoy Sir Thomas Heneage, was the immediate result. The temperature later cooled, but Leicester was recalled before the end of the year.

'Utmost peril' was a trope, indicating anger, rather than a specific threat.

ELIZABETH WROTE:

To my Lord of Leicester from the Queen, by Sir Thomas Heneage.

How contemptuously we conceive ourselves to have been used by you, you shall by this bearer understand; whom we have expressly sent unto you to charge you withal. We could never have imagined (had we not seen it fall out in experience) that a man raised up by ourself and extraordinarily favoured by us, above any other subject of this land, would have in so contemptible a sort broken our commandment in a cause that so greatly touches us in honour. Whereof although you have showed yourself to make but little account in so most undutiful a sort, you may not therefore think that we have so little care of the reparation thereof as we mind to pass so great a wrong in silence unredressed. And therefore our express pleasure and command-ment is that, all delays and excuses laid apart, you do presently upon the duty of your allegiance obey and fulfill whatsoever the bearer hereof shall direct you to do in our name. Whereof fail you not, as you will answer the contrary at your utmost peril.

Leave contemptuously not rewarded of / [...]
to have been by [...] to you, you shall [...]
this to have understood: nyow me have
depeueth, but unto you to require [...]
not all. now could never have imag-
ned (had never not seen it fall out in
experience) that a man rays'd oppo-
sit by the [...] extraordinarily favored by
us, above anie other subiect of this land
would have in so contemptible a sort
broken the commandment in a caust
that so greatly toucheth us in honor:
upon [dekonesty] [...] that you have Sever-
ed [...] to make [but] like attempt in
[...] a sort, you may not [...]
that we have so little care [...] the [...]
tion though at nor mynd to [...] so
great a wrong [...] and [...]
[...] the deepest [...] commandm-
it that, all delays [...] laide
apart, you doe [...] upon the
duty of your allegiance, [...] fullfill
what soever the [...] shall direct you to doe in [...] name: nywr
faile you not as you will answer
the contrary at yor uttarmost perill.

Essex fantasized about himself as a great political patron, and as a leader of armies. In 1589 he tried to join the Norris/Drake expedition to Lisbon without authority, and was recalled in something like disgrace. In 1593 he was given his chance in France at the head of a small expeditionary force, and totally failed to distinguish himself. Having also failed to secure the Principal Secretaryship for his client Francis Bacon, he chose to blame his frustrations on

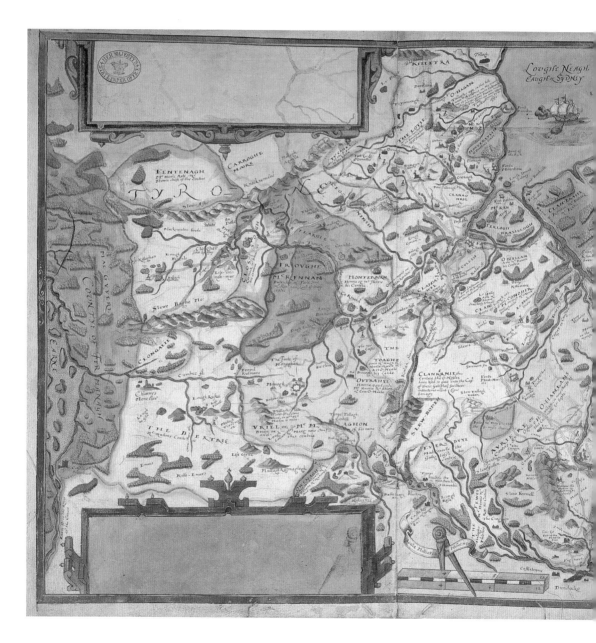

Map of Ulster, Ireland, 1602–3. The scene of the Earl of Tyrone's rebellion.

the Lord Treasurer, Lord Burghley and his son Robert Cecil. Burghley had known the Queen since she was a girl, and had served her loyally for nearly forty years. His relationship with Elizabeth was quite different from Essex's, and absolutely unique. Burghley did not like the younger man, and made his suspicions plain, but it was Essex's own behaviour which undermined him. His greatest success came in his shared leadership of the Cadiz expedition of 1596, but he returned from what could have been a triumph convinced that he had been belittled and ignored, on finding that Robert Cecil had been appointed to the Secretaryship in his absence. Burghley died in 1598, and Elizabeth was deeply affected by the death of her old friend. Essex, quite typically, interpreted her melancholy as an ill humour directed against himself, and sulked publicly.

By 1599 even the Queen was losing patience, but she gave this talented maverick one last chance. She sent him to Ireland as Lord Lieutenant, with a large army to sort out the rebellious Earl of Tyrone. Essex's failure was spectacular. He was out of his depth both politically and militarily, wasted his resources, and finally deserted his post to return to England without leave. Elizabeth was furious (see document 19, *Essex in trouble*); she had him placed under arrest, and the following year deprived him of the sweet wine trading monopoly which was the mainstay of his finances. He blamed Robert Cecil for all his misfortunes, and convinced himself that Elizabeth must be forced to dismiss her secretary and hand him over for trial. With a following of indebted nobles, disappointed place seekers and disgruntled gentleman soldiers, he plotted to seize the court and the Queen's person. Events quickly demonstrated the unreal nature of the world which he inhabited. An attempt to raise London in February 1601 was a complete non-event, and within hours he

A letter from Elizabeth to Robert Devereux, Earl of Essex, in Ireland, 19 July 1599. This is an extract from a clerk's five-page copy.

Between 1594 and 1603 Elizabeth faced her most dangerous challenge: the insurrection in Ireland known as Tyrone's rebellion. Hugh O'Neill, a warlike Irish chieftain, had been made Earl of Tyrone on his submission to Henry VIII in 1542. He was invested with the title and estates in 1587 but soon started plotting with the Irish rebels and the Spanish against Elizabeth.

Essex had been sent to Ireland in the spring of 1599, at the head of a large army and with instructions to bring Tyrone to justice. Instead of driving straight to Ulster and at the Earl of Tyrone, Essex made a senseless progress through Munster. During this time the Earl of Ormond, who was General of Munster in service of the Crown, either forced or persuaded several of his followers and kinsmen, including Baron Cahir (of Cahir Castle, Leinster), to submit to the Queen. The Queen's letter clearly implies that this was all that had been achieved, and

it was small thanks to Essex, who would have considered such people unworthy of his attentions.

After Essex's failure, Elizabeth appointed Charles Blount, Lord Mountjoy, to succeed him. Mountjoy was an experienced soldier who had served in the Low Countries and commanded land forces on the 'islands voyage' to the Azores. It took him three years to bring the campaign to a successful conclusion, but Tyrone finally surrendered in March 1603, just a few days after Elizabeth's death.

ELIZABETH WROTE:

From her majesty to the lord lieutenant.

We have perceived by your letters to our Council brought by Henry Carey that you are arrived at Dublin after your journey into Munster, where though it seems by the words of your letter that you had spent divers days in taking account of all things that have passed since you left that place, yet have you in this dispatch given us small light either when or in what order you intend particularly to proceed to the northern action. Wherein if you compare the time that is run on and in the excessive charges that is spent with the effects of anything wrought by this voyage (howsoever we may remain satisfied with your own particular cares and travails of body and mind), yet you must needs think that we that have the eyes of foreign princes upon our actions and have the hearts of people to comfort and cherish – who groan under the burden of continual levies and impositions which are occasioned by these late actions – can little please ourself hitherto with anything that has been effected.

For what can be more true (if things be rightly examined) than that your two months' journey has brought in never a capital rebel against whom it had been worthy to have adventured one thousand men; for of their two coming-in that were brought unto you by Ormond [Thomas Butler, 10th Earl] (namely Mountgarrett and Cahir) whereupon ensued the taking of Cahir Castle, full well do we know that you would long since have scorned to have allowed it for any great matter in

others to have taken an Irish hold from a rabble of rogues with such force as you had and with the help of the cannon, which were always able in Ireland to make his passage where it pleased. And therefore, more than that, you have now learned upon our expenses, by knowledge of the country, that those things are true which we

The letter continues:

have hitherto told you. If you would have believed us, how far different things would prove from your expectation! There is little public benefit made to us of any things happened in this action which the president [Sir Thomas Norris, Lord President of Munster] with any convenient addition to his numbers by you might not have effected either now or hereafter in a time more seasonable, when it should have less hindered the other enterprise on the which depends our greatest expectation......And where you say further that divers or the most of the voluntary gentlemen are so discouraged thereby, as they begin to desire passports and prepare to return, we cannot as yet be persuaded but that the love of our service and the duty which they owe us have been as strong motives to these their travails and hazards as any affection to the earl of Southampton or any other. If it prove otherwise, which we will not so much wrong ourself as to suspect, we shall have the less cause either to acknowledge or reward it. At the court at Greenwich the nineteenth of July 1599.

20

219

Wee have perceaved by yo(u)r lettr to o(u)r Councell brought
by Henry Cluis, that yo(u) wer arrived at Dublyn after
yo(u)r iourney into Munster, where thoughe it seemeth by the
worder of yo(u)r lre, that yo(u) had spent I ghest tyme in
takinge an accompt of all thinges that have passed synce
yo(u) left that Realm, yet have yo(u) in this dispatch given
that small delight, either when, or in what order yo(u) intend
particulerly to proceed to the northern Action; wherein it
we compare the tyme that is runne on, and the expenc(i)ue
charges that we spent, w(i)th the effects of any thing wrought
by this voyage. Howsoever we may remayne satisffied

1. w(i)th yo(u)r owne perticuler care and travayle of body and
mynd) yet yo(u) must needs thinke, that wee that have
the eyes of forraigne Princes uppon our Action
and have the harts of People to comfort, and cherish,
who grone under the burthen of continuall levyes and
imposicions, wee are wounded by that late Action, we
lyttle please o(u)r self w(i)th w(i)th any thing that hath byn
effected! for what can be more true (of thinges be
rightly examyned) then that yo(u)r two monethes iourney hath
brought in never a Castell Rebell, against whom it thet
byn worthey to have adventured one thousand men; be of their
two commings in, that were brought unto yo(u) by Ormonde
(namely Montgarrett, and Cahyr) whereuppon ensued the
takinge of Cahyr castell, full well do we know that
yo(u) would longe since have scorned to have allowed it for any
great matter in others, to have takin an Irysh hold from a
Rable of Rogues, w(i)th so many stronge as yo(u) had, and w(i)th ye
help of the Cannon, w(i)th were always able in Irelande
to make his passage where it pleased, And therefore more
then that yo(u) have never lerned uppon o(u)r expence, by knowl(edge)
of the Contry, that those thing are true, w(i)th were

826

and his henchmen were in the Tower. From there it was a short and inevitable step to the block, and the Queen was devastated, not by having to enforce the lawful penalty for such an offence, but because her own behaviour had contributed to the tragedy.

Elizabeth had indulged Essex as a silly boy when in fact he had been a wild and dangerous young man. She had tolerated his childish outbursts in a way which no man, least of all her father, would have done. The femininity which in many ways had served her so well, in this case had betrayed her. He had become convinced that he could manipulate her for his own purposes, and when that failed believed that she was being manipulated against him by others. Had she shown her displeasure more firmly, and earlier, none of these dangerous delusions need have arisen. It was noted that she became increasingly melancholy and, about two years after Essex's execution, she died.

QUEEN AND LEGEND

A contemporary view of Elizabeth's funeral cortège, 1603, by William Camden. As with all such royal funerals, a robed effigy of the monarch, sceptre in hand, was placed on top of the coffin. When the monarch's body was removed from view, the effigy remained to provide a tangible representation of the monarchy's 'body politic'.

When Elizabeth died on 24 March 1603, the lamentations were theatrical, but there were also audible sighs of relief – she had become a very difficult old lady. However, the relative failure of her successors magnified her reputation, and she became 'Good Queen Bess', the ever-victorious. No one had quite thought that at the time, in spite of her triumphalist image, but distance lends enchantment to the view. Ultimately, it was to be the use of Elizabethan imagery by the Victorian pioneers of the British Empire which settled the legend in its recent form. Legends are powerful, and facts in themselves, but it is the business of the historian to try to establish the reality.

A copy of Elizabeth's two-page letter to James VI, King of Scots, sent by Mr. Roger Ashton, 4 July 1602.

James's friendship for Elizabeth was based partly upon the fact that they were on the same side in the great ideological struggle of Reformation versus Counter Reformation, but more upon the fact that he was her heir by hereditary right, though he had not been recognized as such. His reaction to his mother's death was restrained for that reason, and he negotiated secretly, first with the Earl of Essex and then with Robert Cecil, to make sure that his claim was established. This was probably not known to Elizabeth, who was extremely sensitive on the subject of the succession. She, however, was anxious to exploit his expectation by maintaining good relations with Scotland during the war with Spain.

In spite of the fact that Henry IV had signed the Treaty of Vervins with Philip II in 1598, by 1602 he was interested in setting up another anti-Spanish coalition, and had just sent an ambassador to James for that purpose. James had immediately informed Elizabeth, and this letter is her response. Henry had expressed considerable admiration for Elizabeth's political skills, and this was not unknown to the Queen. Much of this letter concerns Henry's approach to James, from which it appears that the latter had not been keen to take part in any alliance which did not involve England as well. This was not straightforward, as Elizabeth's Council was very anxious to end the long and stalemated war, so the Queen carefully avoids encouraging such a move. The 'border causes' alluded to in the postscript were the perennial feuds of the clans or 'surnames' on each side of the border, which were steadily being brought under control by the cooperation between London and Edinburgh.

ELIZABETH WROTE:

My good brother,

Who longest draws the thread of life and views the strange accidents that time makes does not find out a rarer gift than thankfulness is, that is most precious and seldomest found. Which makes me well gladded [delighted] that you, methinks, begin to feel how necessary a treasure this is, to be employed where best it is deserved, as may appear in those lines that your last letters express, in which your thanks be great for the sundry cares that of your state and honour my dear friendship has afforded you, being ever ready to give you ever such subjects for your writing, and think myself happy when either my warnings or counsels may in fittest time avail you.

Whereas it has pleased you to impart the offer that the French king has made you, with a desire of secrecy, believe that request includes a trust that never shall deceive, for though many exceeds me in many things, yet I dare profess that I can ever keep taciturnity for myself and my friends. My head may fail, but my tongue shall never, as I will not say but yourself can in yourself, though not to me, witness. But of that no more: *Praetererunt illi dies* [those days will be past]. Now to the French: in plain dealing, without fraud or guile, if he will do as he pretends, you shall be more beholding to him than he is to himself, who within one year has winked at such injuries and affronts as before I would have endured, that am of the weakest sex, I should condemn my judgement. I will not enter into his. And therefore, if his *verba* come *ad actionem* [if his words come to action] I shall more wonder than do suspect; but if you will needs have my single advice, try him if he continue in that mind. And as I know that you would none of such a league as myself should not be one, so do

I see by his overture that himself does; or if for my assistance you should have need of all help, he will give it, so as since he has so good consideration of me, you will allow him therein. And doubt nothing but that he will have me willingly for company; for as I may not forget how their league with Scotland was reciprocated when we had wars with them, so it is good reason that our friendship should be mutual.

Now to confess my kind of taking of all your loving offers and vows of most assured oaths that naught shall be concealed from me that either prince or subject shall, to your knowledge, work against me or my estate; surely, dear brother, you right me much if so you do. And this I vow, that without you list, I will not

The letter continues:

willingly call you in question for such warnings if the greatness of the cause may not compel me thereunto. And I do entreat you to think that if any accident so befall you as either secrecy or speed shall be necessary, suppose yourself to be sure of such a one as shall neglect neither to perform so good a work. Let others promise, and I will do as much with truth as others with wiles. And thus I leave to molest your eyes with my scribbling, with my perpetual prayers for your good estate.

As desires your most loving and affectionate sister

[Postscript] As for your good consideration of border causes, I answer them by my agent, and infinitely thank you therefore.

139

Who longest drawes the thrid of lyfe, and vewes the strange accidents that tyme
makes, doth not fynde out a rarar gift than thankfullnes is, that is most precious
and seldomest found, wch makes me well gladded that you me thinks begins to feele
how necessary a treasure this is to be imployed where best it is deserued, as may appeere
in those lynes that your last lres express, in wch your thanks be greate for the sondry
cares that of your state and honor my deere frendship hath afforded you, being
euer ready to giue you such subiects for your writing, and thinks my self happy
whan eyther my warnings or Counsells may in fittest tyme abayle you. Wheras hit
hath pleased you to impart the offer that ye french king hath made you wt a desire
of secrecy, beleeue that request includes a trust that neuer shall deceaue, for thogh
many exceeds me in many things, yet I dare profess that I can euer keepe tacitur
nitie for my self and my frends. My head may fayle, but my toung
shall neuer, as I will not saye but your self can in yr self, though not so
me, witnes, but of that no more, prætericrunt illi dies. Now to ye frenshe
in playne dealing wout fraude or guile, if he will doo as he pretendes, you
shall be more beholding to him than he is to himself, who wtin one yeere hath
winked at such iniuries and affronts, as or I wold haue endured that an of
the weakest sex, I should condemne my Iudgement, I will not enter into his
And therfore if his verba com ad actiones, I more shall wondar than doo
suspect, but if you will needes haue my single aduise, trye him yf he cotynue
in that mynde. And as I knowe that you wold none of such a league as
my self should not be one, So doo I see by his ouuerture that himself doth
or if for my assistance you should haue neede of all help, he wold
giue it, So as since he hath so good consideraon of me, you will allowe
him therin, and doute nothing but that he will haue me willingly for
company. for as I may not forgett how their league wt Scotland was reci
proke whan we had warres wt them, So is it good reason that our
frendships should be mutuall. Now to cofess my kynde taking of all
your louing offars and vowes of most assured othes that naught shall be
conceled fro me, that eyther Prince or subiect shall to your knowledge
work against me or my estate, Surely deere brother, you right me much
if so you doo, And this I vowe that wout you list, I will not

Who's Who

Catherine of Aragon (1485–1536). Second daughter of Ferdinand of Aragon and Isabella of Castile. Married to Arthur, Prince of Wales, 1501–2, and then to King Henry VIII. Mother of Mary I (born 1516). The marriage was annulled in 1533.

Roger Ascham (1515–68). BA and Fellow of St John's College, Cambridge, 1534; MA 1537. Tutor to Elizabeth, 1548–50. Latin Secretary to Queen Mary, 1553. He married and resigned his Cambridge offices in 1554. Latin Secretary to Elizabeth, 1558. He was the author of *Toxophilus* (1542) and *The Scholemaster* (1570).

Catherine Ashley [née Champernowne] (c.1515–65). Governess, first tutor and Chief Gentlewoman to Elizabeth. Daughter of Sir Philip Champernowne of Devon; married (1545) John Ashley, Gentleman of the Chamber to Henry VIII, and later Master of the Jewel House.

Anthony Babington (1561–86). Gentleman without employment. A former page to Mary, Queen of Scots, he moved to London in about 1580, and was drawn into the Campion circle. He became involved in the conspiracy which bears his name by 1585 and was executed the following year.

Francis Bacon (1561–1626). The younger son of Sir Nicholas Bacon, he was educated at Trinity College, Cambridge (1573–5), and Grays Inn (1576). He was knighted by James I in 1603, and later became Lord Keeper (1617), and Viscount St Albans (1621).

John Bale (1495–1563). A Carmelite of Norwich, he converted to Protestantism in the 1530s, and went abroad after the act of Six Articles (1540–7). He briefly held the Irish see of Ossory in 1553, before going into exile again (1553–9). Later a canon of Canterbury. He was the author of *The Image of Both Churches* (1548).

Henry Bedingfield (1511–83). Of Oxburgh Hall, Norfolk. As Constable of the Tower (1554–5) he had custody of Elizabeth during her imprisonment. Subsequently (1557–8) Vice-Chamberlain and a Privy Councillor. He retired into private life on Elizabeth's accession.

Anne Boleyn (c.1501–36). Mother of Elizabeth; second Queen of Henry VIII; daughter of Thomas Boleyn, Earl of Wiltshire. Executed May 1536 for treasonable adultery and incest.

Thomas Butler, 10th Earl of Ormond (1532–1614). Son of James Butler, 9th Earl. Succeeded as a minor in 1546, and was brought up as a Protestant at the English court. Lord Treasurer of Ireland in 1597, and Lieutenant General of the Army.

Henry Carey, Lord Hunsdon (1524?–96). Son of William Carey, Gentleman of the Privy Chamber to Henry VIII, and Mary Boleyn, Anne's sister. Courtier and soldier. Warden of the East March and Governor of Berwick. Chamberlain of the Household, 1585.

Jean Baptiste Castiglione (no dates). Elizabeth's servant and Italian tutor. Removed from her service in 1556, he was subsequently (1558) a Groom of the Privy Chamber.

Robert Cecil (1563–1612). Second son of William Cecil, Lord Burghley. Trained by his father for the royal service; he became Principal Secretary in 1596, and Lord Keeper of the Privy Seal by 1601. Subsequently Earl of Salisbury (1605) and Lord Treasurer (1608).

William Cecil (1520–98). Principal Secretary 1550–3 and 1558–71. Lord Burghley and Lord Treasurer, 1571–98. Elizabeth's most powerful and influential adviser, and friend over many years. They frequently agreed to disagree over policy.

Charles, Archduke of Austria (c.1540– c.1600). Third son of the Emperor Ferdinand I (reigned 1558–67), and hence a cousin of Philip II. A suitor for Elizabeth's hand, 1563–7.

John Cheke (1514–57). A Greek scholar. BA and Fellow of St John's College, Cambridge, 1529, MA 1533. He was Professor of Greek from 1540 to 1547, and tutor to Prince Edward from 1544. He became Provost of King's College, Cambridge in 1548. He was an MP in 1547 and 1553, and went into exile in the same year. He was captured and imprisoned in 1556, and forced to recant. He died, allegedly of remorse, in the following year.

Thomas Cranmer (1489–1556). Born into a minor gentry family at Aslocton, Notting-hamshire, he matriculated at Jesus College, Cambridge in 1503, taking a BA in 1511 and MA in 1514. He became a fellow of Jesus in 1514, and proceeded BD in 1521. Appointed Archbishop of Canterbury in 1533; he was responsible for first confirming and then annulling Henry VIII's marriage to Anne Boleyn. After 1547 he was the chief architect of Protestant reform. In 1553 he was condemned for treason, but kept in prison until 1555, when he was tried for heresy. He was condemned and burned in March 1556. He was the author of numerous works, including both *Books of Common Prayer* (1549 and 1552).

Thomas Cromwell (1485–1540). Soldier and self-taught lawyer, of obscure origins. He entered Wolsey's service about 1520, and became his secretary in 1525. In 1523 he also became an MP. He entered the King's service from Wolsey's in 1530, and became a Councillor in 1531. He became Master of the Jewel House in 1532, Secretary in 1534, and Lord Privy Seal in 1536. He was the chief architect of the Royal Supremacy, and Vice-Regent in Spirituals. A patron of the reformers, he became Earl of Essex in 1540, and fell victim to a palace revolution in the same year.

Leonard Dacre (d.1573). Second son of William, Lord Dacre of Gilsland. He claimed the Dacre inheritance against the Duke of Norfolk on the death of his nephew in 1569. This may have been the reason he belatedly joined the northern rebellion, hoping for Scottish support. He was defeated and fled, first to Scotland and then to Flanders, where he became a pensioner of Philip II.

Anthony Denny (1501–49). Educated at St Paul's School and St John's College, Cambridge, he entered the King's service before 1540 and became a Gentleman of the Privy Chamber. He was knighted in 1544, and became Groom of the Stool and Chief Gentleman. He was a strong Protestant, and became a Privy Councillor to Edward VI.

Robert Devereux, Earl of Essex (1566–1601). Eldest son of Walter, first Earl of Essex. Inherited as a minor in 1572. His mother, Lettice, remarried Robert Dudley, Earl of Leicester, and Leicester introduced him to the court. From 1588 to 1599 he was Elizabeth's favourite. He commanded armies in France (1593) and Cadiz (1596). He fell from favour as a result of his irresponsible conduct in Ireland in 1599, and blamed his disgrace on Robert Cecil. He attempted a coup against the court in 1601, and was executed.

Francis Drake (c.1525–95). Seaman and adventurer. He was with John Hawkins at San Juan d'Uloa in 1568, and dedicated the rest of his life to fighting Spaniards. His main exploits were his circumnavigation of 1577–80, which earned him his knighthood, and his raid on Cadiz in 1587. He was vice-admiral against the Armada, but fell from favour in the following year, following the Lisbon expedition.

John Dudley, Earl of Warwick and Duke of Northumberland (1502?–53). He was the son of Henry VII's servant Edmund Dudley, and after his father's execution was brought up as a courtier and soldier by Sir Henry Guildford, whose daughter he married. Viscount Lisle and Lord Admiral from 1543, he was an ally of Edward Seymour, and at first supported the Protectorate. In 1549 he turned against Seymour, overthrew him and took power himself. He had great influence over Edward VI, and supported his plan for the succession of Jane Grey. Defeated by Mary in July 1553, he recanted the Protestantism which he had earlier promoted, and was executed for treason.

Robert Dudley, Earl of Leicester (1533–88). Became Earl of Leicester in 1564. Third son of John Dudley (see above). He knew Elizabeth from childhood. Imprisoned after his father's fall, he was released in 1555 and married Amy Robsart (see below). On Elizabeth's accession he became Master of the Horse, and reputedly her lover. In spite of his wife's death in 1560, she decided not to marry him.

Don Gomez Soarez Figueroa, Count of Feria (1520?–71). Agent and confidant of Philip II in England, particularly from 1557 to 1559. After he left England, his household became a refuge for English Catholic fugitives.

John Foxe (1517–87). Graduated from Brasenose College, Oxford, 1538, and was Fellow of Magdalen from 1538 to 1545, when he resigned because of his Protestant convictions. From 1548 to 1553 he was tutor to the children of Henry Howard, Earl of Surrey (executed 1547). In 1554 to fled abroad, returning in 1559. He is best known as a martyrologist and ecclesiastical historian. His *Acts and Monuments of the English Martyrs* went through four editions between 1563 and 1583, and was immensely influential.

François, Duke of Alençon and Anjou (1554–84). Fourth and youngest son of Henri II of France and Catherine de Medici. He was intermittently a candidate for Elizabeth's hand in marriage between 1572 and 1580, and in 1579 she almost decided to marry him. He had plans for intervention in the Netherlands, and was a major nuisance to his brother, Henri III. He died unmarried.

Stephen Gardiner (1497?–1555). Son of John Gardiner, a clothier of Bury St Edmunds. Matriculated at Trinity Hall, Cambridge, in 1511. He proceeded BCL in 1518 and DCL in 1521, taking a doctorate in Canon Law in the following year. He entered Wolsey's service in 1524, and began his diplomatic career in 1527. In 1529 he became the King's secretary, and Bishop of Winchester in 1531. His religious views were conservative, in spite of his support for the Royal Supremacy, and he fell foul of the Protestant governments of Edward VI. He was imprisoned in 1549, and deprived in 1551. Restored by Mary in 1553, he was appointed Lord Chancellor, and played a leading role in initiating the religious persecution which began in 1555.

Jane Grey (1537–54). The eldest daughter of Henry Grey, Marquis of Dorset and Duke of Suffolk (1551), and of Frances, the daughter of Charles Brandon, Duke of Suffolk and his first wife Mary, Henry VIII's sister. Jane was brought up as a Protestant, and her claim to the throne was promoted by Edward VI and the Duke of Northumberland. She was defeated by Mary in a matter of days, convicted of treason, and executed in February 1554.

William Grindal (d.1548). He took a BA from St John's College, Cambridge in 1541, and became a Fellow in 1543. He was tutor to Elizabeth from 1545 to 1548, when he died of plague.

John Hawkins (1532–95). Second son of William Hawkins of Plymouth, merchant and explorer. Apprenticed to the sea. Commanded slaving voyages with the Queen's support to the New World, 1563–8. Treasurer of the Navy, 1577, when he introduced a contract system for ship maintenance. One of Elizabeth's favourite sailors.

Thomas Heneage (d.1595). Eldest son of Robert Heneage of Lincoln, a lawyer. Matriculated at Queen's College, Cambridge, 1549. Treasurer of the Chamber, 1570. Special envoy to the Netherlands, 1586. Vice-Chamberlain of the Household, 1589.

Henri, Duke of Anjou (1551–89). He was the third son of Henri II and Catherine de Medici, and was briefly considered as a husband for Elizabeth (1570–2). A strict Catholic, he refused all religious compromise. He was for a short time the elected king of Poland, but on the death of his brother Charles IX, returned to France as King Henri III. He was assassinated in 1589.

James Hepburn, 4th Earl of Bothwell (c.1535–78). An opponent of the Lords of the Congregation (1558–60) and later of the King-Consort, Lord Darnley. He was generally blamed for the latter's murder in 1567. Officially exonerated and created Duke of Orkney, Queen Mary married him after a staged abduction. He fled abroad after her defeat, and died in prison in Denmark.

Charles Howard, Lord Howard of Effingham (1536–1624). Courtier and cousin of the Queen. He saw sea service from 1570, and was Lord Admiral from 1585 to 1619, during which time he commanded against the Armada. He was created Earl of Nottingham in 1597. His later years were clouded by corruption and inefficiency in the Admiralty.

Thomas Howard, 4th Duke of Norfolk
(1536–72). Eldest son of Henry, Earl of Surrey
(d.1547), he was tutored at home by John Foxe
(see above). He was restored in blood (i.e. his
father's attainder was repealed) and succeeded
his grandfather as Duke of Norfolk in 1554.
He was a member of Elizabeth's Privy Council,
but was imprisoned for plotting to marry Mary
of Scotland (1569–70). Released but out of
favour, he became involved in the Ridolfi plot,
and was executed in 1572.

Henry Lee (1533–1611). A nephew of Thomas
Wyatt the elder, he entered the royal service
in about 1545. He was Clerk of the Armoury,
1549–50, and knighted in 1553. He was
Queen's Champion from 1559 to 1590, and
in that capacity devised the Accession day tilts.
He became Master of the Ordnance in 1590,
and KG in 1597.

Robert Melville (1527–1621). Servant of Mary
Stuart, but was a peacemaker, trusted by both
sides. He became Chancellor of Scotland under
James VI in 1589.

Hugh O'Neill, Earl of Tyrone (1540?–1616).
He was the grandson of Con Breach O'Neill,
and lived in England from 1562 to 1568. He
was set up in Ulster by Elizabeth, and became
defender of the Northern Marches in 1585. He
fell out with the English government and
accepted the hereditary tribal title of The
O'Neill in 1593. The following year he rebelled,
and scored a number of successes in the field
before being defeated by Lord Mountjoy in
1603. He then submitted and renounced his
tribal title, but was never trusted. He fled to
France in 1607, and then to Rome in 1608.
William Overton (1525?–1609). He graduated
from Magdalen College, Oxford in 1539;
became a Fellow in 1551, and proceeded DD

in 1566. A conformist, he held a number of
benefices from 1553, and was appointed Bishop
of Coventry and Lichfield in 1579.

William Paget (1505–63). Lord Paget of
Beaudesert. He was educated at St Paul's School
and Trinity Hall, Cambridge. He served in the
household of Stephen Gardiner, the Bishop of
Winchester, and undertook diplomatic missions
from 1529. He became Clerk of the Council
in 1540, and Secretary of State in 1543. An ally
of Edward Seymour, Earl of Hertford, he was
influential during the latter's Protectorate
(1547–9). He then fell out with the Earl of
Warwick and was imprisoned (1551). Under
Mary he became Lord Privy Seal (1555) but
was dropped by Elizabeth.

Catherine Parr (c.1510–48). Daughter of
Sir William Parr of Kendal. Married Henry VIII
as his sixth wife, and her third husband, in
1543. She subsequently married Lord Thomas
Seymour (1547) and died in childbirth in
September 1548. Evangelical reformer and
friend of Elizabeth.

Thomas Parry (d.1560). Introduced to the court
by his friend, William Cecil, he became first
Elizabeth's Controller, and then her Steward,
before her accession. In 1558 he was appointed
Controller of the Household and Master of
the Wards.

John Piers (1523?–94). He was a fellow of
Magdalen College, Oxford in 1545, and
Senior Student of Christ Church in 1547.
He proceeded MA in 1549 and DD in 1566.
He was elected Master of Balliol in 1570, and
appointed Bishop of Rochester in 1576. From
there he was translated to Salisbury in 1577,
and York in 1589.

Alvarez de Quadra, Bishop of Aquila
(c.1510–53). Philip II's first ambassador
in England. His desire to help the English
Catholics and to promote the faith was
constantly getting in the way of his diplomatic
mission. He favoured the marriage negotiation
with Archduke Charles, and died in post
in 1563.

Simon Renard (c.1520–73). A gentleman
of Franche-Compté, and a career diplomat.
He was Charles V's ambassador in England
from 1553 to 1555, and was largely responsible
for negotiating the marriage treaty between
Philip and Mary. He disliked and distrusted
Elizabeth, and tried to persuade Mary to
execute her.

Roberto Ridolfi (1531–1612). A Florentine
merchant who settled in London early in
Elizabeth's reign. Did business with William
Cecil. He seems to have been largely responsible
for the conspiracy in favour of Mary of Scotland
which bears his name. When it was detected,
he returned to Florence, where he became
a senator in 1600.

Amy Robsart (1532?–60). The daughter of
Sir John Robsart of Norfolk, she married Robert
Dudley in 1555. Her death (probably of breast
cancer) in 1560 caused an immense scandal,
because it was believed that Robert had had
her murdered in order to marry the Queen.
Edward Seymour, Earl of Hertford and Duke
of Somerset (c.1506–52). He was the brother
of Henry VIII's third Queen, Jane Seymour.
A successful courtier, he was created Earl in
1537, and subsequently pursued a military
career, commanding in Scotland in 1544.
He belonged to the reforming party at court
in Henry's last years, and seized control of the

regency government after his death, becoming
Duke and Lord Protector. He was overthrown
in a coup in October 1549, and executed three
years later.

Jane Seymour (1509?–37). The daughter of Sir
John Seymour of Wolf Hall, near Marlborough.
She was a gentlewoman to Queen Anne Boleyn,
and after Anne's execution, Henry VIII's third
wife. In October 1537 she gave birth to Prince
Edward, and died a few days later. She was a
woman of no particular opinions, and Henry's
favourite wife.

Thomas Seymour, Baron Seymour of Sudeley
(c.1510–49). He was the younger brother of
Edward, and his jealous rival. He succeeded in
marrying the Queen Dowager (Catherine Parr)
in 1547, and after her death in 1548, sought
to marry Elizabeth. For that, for his
misdemeanours as Lord Admiral, and for
conspiring against the Protector, he was arrested
in January 1549, and condemned by Act of
Attainder.

Jean de Simier (no dates). A skilled courtier,
he was the Duke of Anjou's agent for dealing
with Elizabeth. He became something of a
favourite with her, but fell out of favour with
his master by 1579.

Henry Stuart, Lord Darnley, Earl of Ross,
Duke of Albany (1545–67). He was the
eldest son of Matthew Stuart, Earl of Lennox,
and Margaret [Douglas], the daughter of
Margaret Tudor by her second marriage to
Archibald, Earl of Angus. Exiled with his father
in England, he returned with him in 1565.
Having received his new titles, he married
Mary, Queen of Scots in July 1565, and was

the father of James VI and I. As King-Consort he was controversial and unpopular. He was murdered at Kirk o' Fields in February 1567.

Francis Walsingham (c.1530–90). Educated at King's College, Cambridge (1548) and Gray's Inn (1552). An exile for religion in Mary's reign, he entered the service of William Cecil in about 1565, as an intelligence agent. He undertook several diplomatic missions, and was appointed Principal Secretary in 1573. As Secretary, he ran Elizabeth's counter-espionage service. He was knighted in 1577.

John Whitgift (c.1530–1604). Educated at St Anthony's School, London, and Pembroke Hall, Cambridge. He took a BA in 1554, and MA in 1557, becoming a Fellow of Peterhouse in 1555. He was ordained in 1560, and became Lady Margaret Professor of Divinity in 1563. He became Master of Trinity College in 1567, and Vice-Chancellor in 1570, during which time he conducted a long dispute with the Presbyterian Thomas Cartwright. He was appointed Bishop of Worcester in 1577, and Archbishop of Canterbury in 1583. He was the only bishop to serve on Elizabeth's Privy Council.

Thomas Williams (1513?–66). Trained at the Inner Temple, where he was entered in 1539, and was the Lent Reader in 1558. He was an MP in 1555, 1558 and 1563, and was appointed Speaker in the latter year.

William Winter (d.1589). He was the son of a Bristol merchant, and was apprenticed to the sea. In naval service by 1544, he became Surveyor of the Navy in 1549, and Master of the Naval Ordnance in 1557. He was subsequently a vice-admiral, and served as such against the Armada.

Thomas Wyatt (1521–54). He was the son of the courtier poet of the same name, and was a Kentish landowner, magistrate and part-time soldier. He became involved in a conspiracy to thwart Mary's plans to marry Philip of Spain, and led a rebellion for that purpose in January 1554. He was defeated, and executed in April.

John Young (1534?–1605). He graduated at Pembroke Hall, Cambridge, BA in 1552, MA in 1555. He was ordained in 1561, and proceeded BD in 1563. Elected Master of Pembroke Hall in 1567, he became both DD and Vice-Chancellor in 1569, and was appointed Bishop of Rochester in 1578.

Chronology

1533	7 September Birth of Elizabeth.
1536	17 May Execution of Anne Boleyn.
	18 July Elizabeth declared illegitimate by statute.
1537	14 October Elizabeth attends Edward's christening.
1540	28 July Execution of Thomas Cromwell.
1543	12 May Elizabeth included in the Act of Succession.
	12 July Henry VIII marries his last Queen, Catherine Parr. The reforming party recovers the initiative at court.
1545–8	Elizabeth resident in Queen Catherine's household.
1547	28 January Death of King Henry VIII.
1548	First advances made by Thomas Seymour; Elizabeth sent away from the Seymour household.
	5 September Death of Catherine, the Queen Dowager. Seymour proposes marriage to Elizabeth.
1549	January Arrest of Thomas Seymour.
	January–February Catherine Ashley and Elizabeth interrogated about Seymour.
	March Execution of Thomas Seymour.
	9 October Overthrow of Edward Seymour, Duke of Somerset, Lord Protector.
1551	Elizabeth takes control of the estates allocated to her under the terms of her father's will.
1553	6 July Death of Edward VI. Lady Jane Grey is proclaimed Queen in London, and both Mary and Elizabeth are excluded from the succession.
	19 July Jane's claim not supported; Mary proclaimed Queen. Elizabeth joins her in London.

1553   September Elizabeth forced to attend Mass.

1554   January Sir Thomas Wyatt leads a rebellion in Kent against the Queen's proposed marriage to Philip II of Spain.

                10 February Elizabeth arrested for suspected complicity in the rebellion.

                12 February Jane Grey and Guildford Dudley executed.

                18 March Elizabeth committed to the Tower of London.

                20 May Elizabeth sent into house arrest at Woodstock.

1555   May Elizabeth brought to court for Mary's lying-in. Released in August.

1556   March Elizabeth compromised by the Dudley conspiracy. Her household placed under new management.

1556–7   Philip attempts to marry Elizabeth to the Duke of Savoy.

1558   June The Count of Feria visits her in secret.

                17 November Death of Mary; Elizabeth succeeds her.

1559   8 May Acts of Supremacy and Uniformity become law.

                November The Scottish Lords of the Congregation seek her support.

1559–61   Elizabeth's love affair with Robert Dudley.

1560   February Treaty of Berwick with the Lords of the Congregation.

                July Treaty of Edinburgh. The French withdraw from Scotland.

1562   October Elizabeth dangerously ill with smallpox.

1562–3   Unsuccessful intervention in France.

1563–7   Negotiations for marriage with the Archduke Charles.

1564   Calais finally relinquished by the Treaty of Troyes.

1568   May Mary, Queen of Scots arrives in England.

1568	December Elizabeth borrows Genoese money destined for the Duke of Alba. Embargo on trade with the Low Countries.
1569	November Rebellion of the northern earls.
1570	February Leonard Dacre defeated.
1570–1	Search for a French alliance leads to negotiations for a marriage with Henri of Anjou.
1571–2	Ridolfi plot involves Mary, Queen of Scots. There is pressure to bring her to trial.
1572	21 April Treaty of Blois signed with France.
	2 June Duke of Norfolk executed.
	August St Bartholomew's Eve massacres in France.
1572–8	Marriage negotiations with François, Duke of Anjou.
1575	17 May Death of Matthew Parker, Archbishop of Canterbury.
1577–80	Francis Drake circumnavigates the world.
1579–81	Second (and final) negotiation for a marriage with François, Duke of Anjou.
1583	23 September John Whitgift becomes Archbishop of Canterbury.
1585	17 August Treaty of Nonsuch with the United Provinces. De facto war with Spain.
1585–6	Francis Drake raids the West Indies.
1586	The Babington conspiracy implicates Mary, Queen of Scots.
	November Trial and conviction of Mary, Queen of Scots.
1587	8 February Execution of Mary, Queen of Scots.
	April–June Drake raids Cadiz.
1588	August Spanish Armada defeated.

1588   September Death of the Earl of Leicester.

1589   Francis Drake and Sir John Norris fail at Lisbon.

            Henri III of France assassinated. Henri of Navarre becomes Henri IV.
            Civil wars continue.

1593   Elizabeth intervenes in Normandy and Brittany against the Catholic League.

1594   7 November Sir John Norris captures the fort of Blavet in Brittany.

            Beginning of the Earl of Tyrone's rebellion in Ulster.

1595   Francis Drake and John Hawkins die on an expedition to the New World.

1596   June The Earl of Essex and Lord Admiral Charles Howard capture
            and sack Cadiz.

            15 July Sir Robert Cecil becomes Principal Secretary.

1597   Failure of the Earl of Essex's expedition to the Azores (the 'Islands' voyage).

1598   4 August Death of William Cecil, Lord Burghley.

1599   The Earl of Essex fails in Ireland. Returns without leave, and is placed
            under arrest.

1601   February Revolt of the Earl of Essex.

            25 February Execution of the Earl of Essex.

            30 November The 'golden speech' to Parliament.

1603   The Earl of Tyrone submits to Lord Mountjoy.

            24 March Death of Elizabeth.

Further Reading

Simon Adams, *Leicester and the Court* (Manchester University Press, 2002). A collection of essays, most of them previously published, but amended and updated.

Stephen Alford, *The Early Elizabethan Polity* (Cambridge University Press, 1998). A thoroughly researched discussion of the ideas and working practices of Sir William Cecil in the 1560s: good on the British dimension.

Philippa Berry, *Of Chastity and Power* (Routledge, 1989). Explores the literature of the Virgin Queen; the origin and effectiveness of the image.

J. B. Black, *The Reign of Elizabeth* (Clarendon Press, 1950). An old fashioned narrative history of the reign: a mine of information, although some of the interpretations are outdated.

Susan Doran, *Monarchy and Matrimony: The Courtships of Elizabeth I* (Routledge, 1996). Exhaustively researched account of the foreign policy aspects of Elizabeth's courtships, from 1558 to 1581.

John Guy ed., *The Reign of Elizabeth I: Court and Culture in the Last Decade* (Cambridge University Press, 1995). Discusses the declining years of Elizabeth's image and the search for a replacement.

Norman Jones, *Faith by Statute: Parliament and the Settlement of Religion, 1559* (Royal Historical Society, 1982). The best account of the parliamentary politics of the Elizabethan settlement; argues that Elizabeth got what she wanted against the opposition of the Lords.

Norman Jones, *The Birth of the Elizabethan Age: England in the 1560s* (Blackwell, 1993). General account of the politics of the first decade; good on the French and Scottish interventions.

David Loades, *The Chronicles of the Tudor Queens* (Sutton, 2002). Extracts from documents, with a brief commentary, covering the period 1553–1603.

Wallace MacCaffrey, *The Shaping of the Elizabethan Regime, 1558–1572* (Jonathan Cape, 1969). Slightly dated but very thorough account of every aspect of early Elizabethan politics; good on deteriorating relations with Spain, and the Northern Rebellion.

Wallace MacCaffrey, *Queen Elizabeth and the Making of Policy, 1572–1588* (Princeton University Press, 1981). Mid-Elizabethan politics; good on the affairs of the Netherlands, relations with France, and seafaring.

Leah S. Marcus, Janel Mueller and Mary B. Rose, eds., *Elizabeth I: Collected Works* (University of Chicago Press, 2000). Invaluable collection of Elizabeth's own writings, covering speeches, letter, prayers and poems written during the whole length of her life. Particularly good on relations with the Duke of Anjou, and Mary, Queen of Scots.

Sir John Neale, *Elizabeth I and her Parliaments* (2 vols., Jonathan Cape, 1955, 1957). The standard account and a very good narrative. Many of his interpretations have been challenged, but some of the revisers are now themselves being revised.

Conyers Read, *Mr Secretary Cecil and Queen Elizabeth* (Jonathan Cape, 1955). Exhaustive, and not easy reading, but firmly based on the voluminous sources. Should now be read in conjunction with Alford.

David Starkey, *Elizabeth* (Vintage, 2001). Breezy, well written account of Elizabeth's early life, containing some valuable insights. Unreferenced.

R. B. Wernham, *After the Armada* (Oxford University Press, 1984). The most thorough account of the last fifteen years of the reign; good on the war and seafaring.

Derek Wilson, *Sweet Robin: A Biography of Robert Dudley, Earl of Leicester, 1533–1588* (Hamish Hamilton, 1981). Still the best full biography of this important figure, but should now be read in conjunction with Adams.

Picture Credits

Illustrations

Cover and p. 34 National Portrait Gallery, London, UK/Bridgeman Art Library; pp. i and 80 Courtesy of The Marquess of Salisbury; p. 3 Ashmolean Museum, Oxford, UK/Bridgeman Art Library; p. 4 Courtesy of the National Portrait Gallery, London; p. 8 Helmingham Hall, Suffolk, UK/Bridgeman Art Library/Mark Fiennes; p. 9 The Royal Collection © 2003 Her Majesty Queen Elizabeth II; p. 10 National Portrait Gallery, London, UK/Bridgeman Art Library; p. 15 Courtesy of the National Portrait Gallery, London; p. 22–3 The Royal Collection, 2003, Her Majesty Queen Elizabeth II; p. 26 left, Prado, Madrid, Spain/Bridgeman Art Library; p. 28 Private Collection/Bridgeman Art Library; p. 32 The Royal Collection, Her Majesty Queen Elizabeth II; p. 33 Collections/John D Beldom; p. 38 The Art Archive/College of Arms/Eileen Tweedy; p. 39 Burghley House Collection, Lincolnshire, UK/Bridgeman Art Library; p. 42 Wallace Collection, London, UK/Bridgeman Art Library; p. 47 Lambeth Palace Library, London, UK/Bridgeman Art Library; p. 50 Private Collection/Bridgeman Art Library; pp. 52–3 © Staatliche Museen Kassel, Germany; p. 54 Hermitage, St Petersburg, Russia/Bridgeman Art Library; p. 66 Victoria & Albert Museum, London, UK/Bridgeman Art Library; p. 72 Collections/Archie Young; pp. 76–7 by permission of the British Library (MS Harley 290, f. 203); p. 89 Ashmolean Museum, Oxford, UK/Bridgeman Art Library; p. 93 Woburn Abbey, Bedfordshire, UK/Bridgeman Art Library; pp. 100–1 British Library, London, UK/Bridgeman Art Library.

All other images are from The National Archives:
Cover and p. 2 KB 27/1289/2;
cover (background) SP 78/48 f. 167;
p. ii KB 27/1241/2; p. iii SC 13/N3;
p. v KB 27/1309/2; p. x E 36/277;
pp. 4–5 E 344/22; p. 7 KB 8/9;
p. 20 KB 27/1150/2; p. 25 KB 8/23;
p. 26 right, KB 27/1168/2;
p. 27 KB 27/1185/2; p. 55 MPF 1/6;
p. 60 MPF 1/318; p. 61 SP 9/205/1;
p. 69 MPF 1/366, extract from SP 52/13;
p. 73 SP 52/13/60; pp. 82–3 MPB 1/23;
pp. 84, 85 KB 27/1276/2; p. 88 MPEE 1/25;
p. 96 MPF 1/36

Picture research by Deborah Pownall.

Original documents

Document 1, by permission of the Bodleian Library; document 9, by courtesy of The Marquess of Salisbury; documents 15 & 18, by permission of the British Library; document 17, by permission of the Syndics of Cambridge University Library. *On Monsieur's Departure*, transcribed with document 17, is held at the Bodleian Library, MS Tanner 76, f. 94r. All other documents are held in The National Archives.

Document transcripts

The author gratefully acknowledges the use of *Elizabeth I: Collected Works*, eds L. S. Marcus, J. Mueller and M. B. Rose (Chicago University Press, 2000) for the transcripts of documents 1, 2, 3, 4, 5, 6, 8, 9, 10, 13, 14, 16, 17, 18, 19, 20; and *Tudor Royal Proclamations*, Vol II by P. L. Hughes and J. F. Larkin (Yale University Press, 1969) for document 15.

Index

Page references to illustrations are in *italics*; page references to documents are in **bold**.